LAKE | FLATO HOUSES

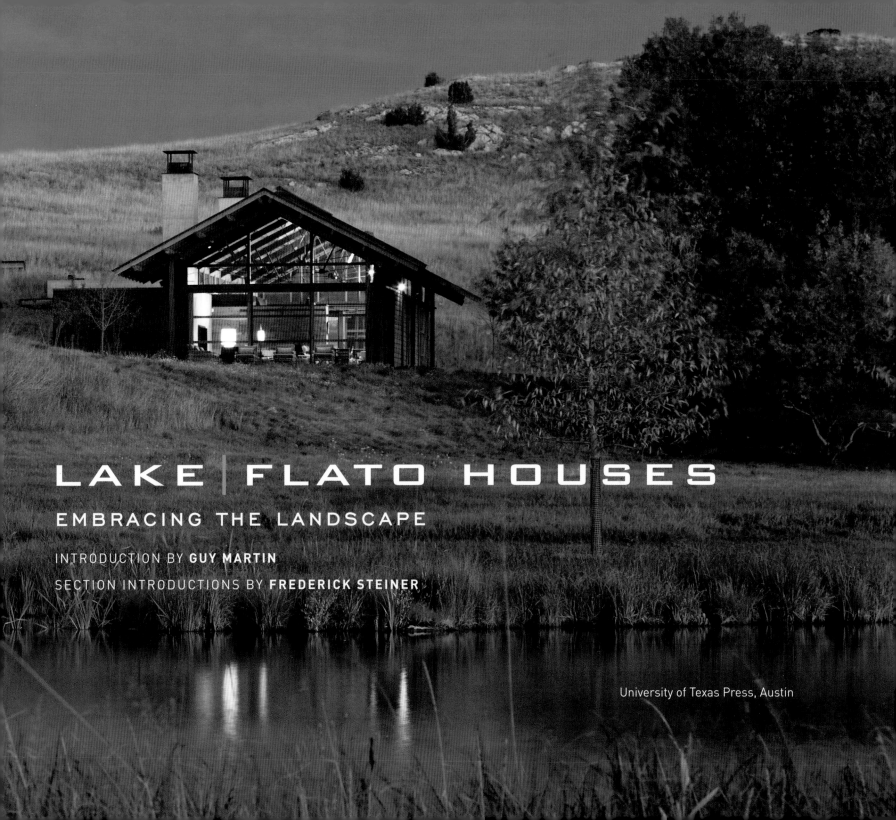

LAKE | FLATO HOUSES

EMBRACING THE LANDSCAPE

INTRODUCTION BY **GUY MARTIN**

SECTION INTRODUCTIONS BY **FREDERICK STEINER**

University of Texas Press, Austin

This book was supported in part by the University of Texas Press Advisory Council.

LIBRARY OF CONGRESS CATALOGING-IN-PUBLICATION DATA

Lake|Flato houses : embracing the landscape / introduction
by Guy Martin ; section introductions by Frederick Steiner.
— First edition.
      pages   cm
ISBN 978-0-292-75845-2 (pbk. : alk. paper)
1. Lake/Flato (Firm) 2. Architecture, Domestic—Texas—
History—21st century.
NA737.L25A4 2014
728′.370922—dc23   2013038463

doi:10.7560/758452

We believe that architecture must be a partner with the environment: where the landscape and buildings are an inseparable team; where the forms, as with early vernacular structures, are shaped by the climate; where the materials are of the place; where science and technology are combined with art and craft.

For thirty years, Lake|Flato has been a passionate advocate for environmental stewardship through sustainable design. We are committed to the 2030 Architecture Challenge, and our in-house Sustainability Team ensures that our projects make the critical connection between design intent and actual building performance to measure progress toward carbon-neutral buildings.

LAKE|FLATO ARCHITECTS

CONTENTS

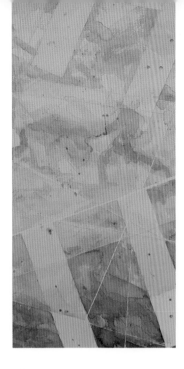
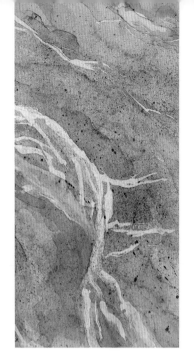
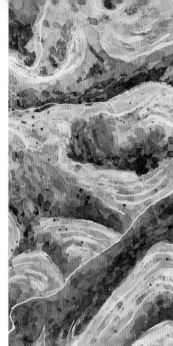

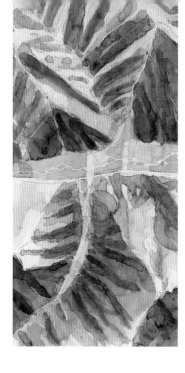  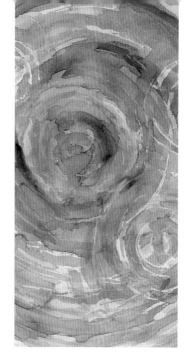

PREFACE

When we decided to create our own architecture firm in 1984, we had a number of strong ideas about the kind of buildings we wanted to design. We believed first and foremost that architecture should be rooted in its particular place, responding in a meaningful way to the natural or built environment. Using local materials and partnering with the best local craftsmen, we sought to create buildings that were tactile and modern, environmentally responsible and authentic, artful and crafted.

Thirty years later these beliefs still inform the architecture we create. While our firm has grown along with the range and complexity of our projects, we have found the desire to build in partnership with the land to be an approach that continues to be purposeful and is increasingly resonant. Our first projects were houses, and these projects excite us still. We have found that by exploring the intimate relationships among

family, place, and building, we can create unique living environments that possess a compelling authenticity and beauty. While architects may traditionally be known as the designers of buildings alone, we see buildings as merely one piece of a much larger picture. In our houses, the architecture and landscape are one—with outdoor rooms and courtyards becoming as important as the enclosed interior spaces. Often these interior spaces open up to the outdoors, creating a hybrid space and blurring the distinction between indoors and out.

By designing in harmony with the land, we create designs that, by their massing, orientation, and materials, are inherently sustainable. Light overhanging roofs keep direct sunlight out of windows and can also be designed to collect rainwater or solar energy. Massive stone walls help absorb radiant energy, keeping interiors cool during

Lasater House, Fort Worth, Texas (1984), with its floating pavilions, is a
good example of a structure that partners with its natural environment.

the day and warm at night. We increasingly use building performance simulation software to test assumptions and to develop designs that optimize energy use. While emerging technologies help provide additional layers of science, our initial concepts are often based on a passive climatic response inspired by the vernacular structures of the region. Built before mechanical systems could provide hot and cold air, these early pragmatic structures provide invaluable lessons today in how a building can harvest daylight and rainwater while protecting against harsh winter winds and blistering summer sun. These buildings are sustainable, practical, timeless, and beautiful, and continue to inform our design process.

While we certainly take pride in the buildings that have resulted from these efforts, we perhaps derive the greatest sense of accomplishment from the team of talented and driven individuals we have assembled at Lake|Flato. Our office "family" shares a common set of values. We love what we do, and, while the work itself is rewarding, so too are the people we work with every day.

As important as collaboration is within our office, we also highly value working with engineers, contractors, and craftsmen, each of whom is critical to the ultimate success of any project. Their knowledge of systems performance and how buildings are constructed and maintained is integral to the design of each project and leads to sustainable, practical, and artful homes.

The other important team member is, of course, the client. Over the years, we have been fortunate to have the opportunity to work with individuals, couples, and families who have supported, inspired, and challenged us. In working with our clients to realize their dreams, we have been given the opportunity to realize our own. —LAKE|FLATO ARCHITECTS

As friend and mentor Bill Turnbull writes in our first monograph:

Lake|Flato Architects have specifically Texas insights, but the quality of their translation into architecture can serve as a lesson for us all: how a building stands to the sun, how it welcomes the cooling breeze, how it partners with plant materials: these are lessons in siting. Appropriate construction materials are important so the structure marries with the site: corrugated iron to turn away the heat, heavy stone or adobe to shelter the occupants, light frame for the support of shady porches, cool tile for floors underfoot. Nothing sensational or exotic, no visual fireworks of fashion, just architecture that intrigues the mind, delights the soul, and refreshes the eye with its elegant detail and simplicity.

Timeless architecture needn't shout; it is more pleasant to listen to the wind whispering through it.

WILLIAM TURNBULL, FAIA (1996)

From the foreword to Lake|Flato's first monograph, *Contemporary World Architects*

LAKE | FLATO HOUSES

INTRODUCTION

GUY MARTIN

Alamo Cement House, Kyle, Texas (1990), incorporates a recycled steel-framed "shed" from a cement plant in San Antonio.

Founding partner David Lake and I are sitting in a conference room in the bustling Lake|Flato offices, located in a former 1930s automobile dealership two hundred yards northeast of the Alamo. From this spot in March of 1836, one of General Santa Anna's batteries rained down some pretty good cannon fire on Bowie's and Travis's back door.

Lake and I are discussing the sea change that America's builders, manufacturers, and architects underwent in the late 1990s, as the economic and environmental benefits of "green" building materials and practices began to be realized. Sustainability ratings for buildings did not exist, nor did the ratings agency, the U.S. Green Building Council. Lake|Flato had been in existence for fifteen years, and had become locally renowned for its resolute strategy of reducing the energy demands of its public and private buildings, cheating the blazing Texas sun, eschewing air conditioning when shade or wind would do, adding porches and plazas, shading walls, and generally coaxing its clients to open their buildings to the out-of-doors. But there were no real rules.

"The University of Texas School of Nursing came to us in 1998 and said, 'We want a sustainable nursing school that will be a nurturing place for the people who work inside it and that will also help the community around it,'" Lake explains. "So we teamed with the Houston office of Berkebile, Nelson, Immenschuh, and McDowell to make that building as 'friendly,' meaning as efficient, as possible. But that was the moment when the various technologies and metrics were at a point so that, with enough study, we could start really grinding down on the numbers to make our houses work to be more efficient. It's when it became possible to systematize what we'd been doing."

The architecture of Texas looks a lot different now than it did when the Republic was founded in 1836, but the state's topography and infamous climatic extremities are intact. In the east, the same hurricane-lashed Gulf swamps give way to dry, hilly chaparral. In the southern and western reaches of the state, the Chihuahuan desert is still the vengeful ruling god: the temperature reaches a hundred for a hundred days a year, and the annual rainfall is less than twelve inches. The Panhandle's

prairies still have the highest annual concentration of tornadoes of any region on the North American continent.

For people, animals, and buildings in Texas, the fight is to survive all that. The architects designing each structure built on this ground—be it a gas station in Del Rio, a glass office tower in Houston, or the oasis-like El Tule, the South Texas ranch house on the following page—must still pick their way through many of the challenges that the early settlers faced.

"The lesson we've learned," Lake says drily, one hundred and seventy-eight years after the Battle of the Alamo, "is that if you can build in Texas, you can build anywhere."

Much of the joy of looking at Lake|Flato's work, collected in the following pages, is to watch these homes respond to their respective landscapes. They may seem to be tucked into this or that fold of the earth, but they are not sedentary dwellings. They put their inhabitants in the land, protect them, elevate them, light them in the day, cloak them at night, make them move, let them rest. Taken as a whole, these houses know their footing, they flow into the landscape, they hew to the contours like horses—here's a surefooted pony that's good in the mountains, here's one that knows how to stay low and run long in the chaparral. Each one has a different set of muscles and a different gait.

Texas landscapes.

El Tule Ranch, Falfurrias, Texas (1992). Responds to the challenges of the hot South Texas climate with its oasis-like courtyard.

The houses in this book come by that trademark resilience honestly. Partner Bob Harris, a United States Green Building Council (USGBC) Fellow, has made sustainability his personal focus within the firm. He has been been instrumental in applying cutting-edge analytics and building technologies—in materials and in the mechanical systems of the buildings—to each project. Woven into the design process now are reams of analysis by a team of engineers who pore over the siting, heating, and cooling requirements of the structures.

"Our early projects were based on an intuitive approach to energy conservation, and now, with more science applied, we can go further," Harris says. "We can take a house to net zero with many passive-gain strategies and materials. We can also take it entirely off the grid. Every house is now 'smart' to a certain level, but beyond that the level of science we apply is largely determined by how the client wants to live, and in what kind of environment."

In the eighteenth century, the Spanish colonial response to the intense heat in their precincts of Texas was to build the fat-walled New World baroque adobe missions and their secular cousins, the haciendas. The stone and stucco had moderately good insulating properties, and the windows were shuttered, which also helped combat the heat. The operative notion was that the world was so angry that it must be walled out—a pre-air-conditioning attempt at air-conditioning philosophy. Some of the roofs of the adobe

La Barronena Ranch, Hebronville, Texas (1986). With more porch
than house, it takes advantage of the cool coastal breezes.

dwellings were flat, occasionally with parapets, and some were hipped and tiled. The walls did keep out some heat, but one could also make the argument that the Spanish were slowly roasting themselves in variously shaped clay ovens.

In the first third of the nineteenth century, the Spanish colonial idiom was subjected to a very different architectural influence, namely, that of the English and German settlers. Houses, in the German and the English view, required a knockabout clapboard sort of openness, higher ceilings, bigger windows—features consciously designed to catch a breeze. Buildings were stripped down because ornament was frippery, and there was no room for frippery in Texas.

The early settlers from the next-door parts of the Deep South, where the weather was humid and the breeze highly prized, pushed westward into East Texas with the classic dogtrot house: two rooms, separated by a central open hall, covered by a tin roof whose ridge often paralleled the road—or, more precisely, was sited so that the breeze could draw through the open hall, as if the wind were the trotting dog for which the style of house was named.

The settlers quickly discovered that there was wood in the Piney Woods and in the Hill Country, but there wasn't enough to fill the needs of a state the size of Texas. The place was rich in limestone, much of South Texas having been a marshy sea back in the Pleistocene. As the industrialized twentieth century arrived and

Working with local forms and materials. Top: Airbarns (1997), built of recycled oil-field pipe. Bottom: Limestone road cut.

manufacturing technology was brought to bear on agriculture, there was an increasing use of steel in ranching operations, in barn structures for livestock, fencing, silos, pumps, troughs, and windmills.

The second great catalyst for the universal presence of steel in Texas was oil production. The huge new East Texas field, the most productive in America to this day, came online in the late 1930s, just as World War II was creating a huge spike in the need for petroleum. Over the last seventy years, Texas has had a need for every sort of engineering and fabricating talent, carpenters, and stonemasons, and welders who can run a bead so true that it is difficult to understand the alchemy that brought the seam about.

The palette of the seventy-three Lake|Flato architects and engineers whose excellent work we see on the following pages comes straight out of that history and these materials: stone, steel, wood, harsh weather, and the fine and eclectic mix of architectural vernacular styles from various local communities, both residential and industrial. The influences are clear, as seen in the use of recycled oil-field pipe on the barn in San Saba and the drilled and squared rock face on the previous page. But there's a big difference between staring at a weathered limestone face on the westbound side of I-10 (p. 7) and employing the delicate calculus to figure out how that stone might best be used on *this* hillside, in *this* piece of *that* house.

It's no exaggeration to say that Ted Flato has rocks in his head—many extraordinary rocks, a catalogue of indigenous Tex-Mex geology, in fact. His knowledge, curated by his use of and experiences with the material over the last thirty years, is a lovely thing. But to explain the rock catalogue's depth and breadth, we must take another step back.

Lake|Flato had its beginnings in the San Antonio offices of the iconic Texas architect O'Neil Ford, where, in the late 1970s, Lake, Flato and a number of the architects who would eventually form the firm met and worked. Ford was an iconoclast, a resolutely "local" architect enamored of no fashion except what felt right, as defined by the landscape and the materials at hand. Largely self-taught, he was awarded the National Medal of Arts and was, curiously, the only human ever to be designated a National Historic Landmark. Late in his career, Ford was the absolute enemy of what he considered the overly mannered postmodernists.

"He came to work one day, disgusted with the way contemporary architecture was headed," says Flato, "and announced that he was going to call himself a 'premodernist.'"

Ford was simply and brilliantly original. It's fair to say that Fordian architectural DNA has infused itself into the fabric of the Lake|Flato approach. Upon Ford's death in 1983, Flato and Lake spun off and formed their firm.

O'Neil Ford, friend and mentor, in his San Antonio office circa 1980.

Chandler Ranch, Mason, Texas (1993). With dry-stacked local limestone that seems to grow out of the hillside.

"For years at O'Neil's firm we used what we called Ol' Yella, a beautiful buff limestone that we could only get from this angry old German rancher named Seidensticker," Flato explains. "The supplier was Charlie Cade. He was difficult, too. Cade had the quarry. You'd go out there and he'd say, "Welp, hit's been rainin'. Got nothin' for ya.' Three weeks would go by. You'd go out there. He'd say, 'Welp, sorry.' But Ol' Yella came off in these gorgeous four-inch-thick slabs, real big, you could do anything with them. We put them on the House of Courts in San Antonio. I think that might have been the last time we used that limestone."

That house (pp. 12, 14), clad in those delightfully massive three-foot-tall slabs of Seidensticker's best Ol' Yella, has a kind of Middle Eastern grace. The size of the slabs gives the house great permanence, and yet—as you sit by the lap pool and regard the courtyard—there's a light, cool quality, too, as if the house is wearing a crisp, dun-colored linen suit.

"But that," Flato says, "is not really the best stone. There's this *other*, truly magical stone from Mexico. One day, when we were still working for O'Neil, I was trying to figure out what to use on a house, and O'Neil took a look and said, 'You need Vallecillo.' 'What's that?' I said. He said, 'There's this little town down in Mexico, south of Laredo but not all the way to Monterrey. You should go take a look.' And that's all he said."

House of Courts, San Antonio, Texas (1997). Large blocks of Ol' Yella limestone give it an Old World grace.

Flato drove down to Vallecillo. The stone was an extraordinarily rich tan with a gray interior, and had not gone unnoticed by the locals. Most of the public buildings and many of the houses were clad in the stuff.

"The thing that made it so special was that something happened to that stone back in the Pleistocene," Flato explains. "What happened was that the seas ebbed and flooded. Each time the Gulf of Mexico covered this area, a different sediment of limestone would be added—and each time it ebbed, a layer of dry caliche would be added that prevented the layers of limestone from attaching to each other, which gave us the two weathered faces, on the top

Karla Greer, Vallecillo, Mexico (1980), just after the discovery of the "miracle stone."

and the bottom of each sediment. There were also these vertical fissures that went down through the layers, and as the ocean receded, the caliche would fill those, too. The result was a stone with four beautiful, weathered faces. It had such tremendous authority, that rock. We bought truckloads of it."

What's so striking—thirty-three years on—is the specificity of it all: under this one village outside Monterrey were these rich sediments of limestone that an extraordinary series of geophysical accidents lapped and laid atop each other over million of years, resulting in a bit of natural beauty harnessed by O'Neil Ford, who then years later passed the tip along at one moment in time to one young architect, who then covered a client's house in Laredo in this stone. This is an architectural chain of events that reaches back, grabs the prehistoric world and brings it into the present, as if the stone under Vallecillo had never been buried and the intervening 20 million years were an eyeblink.

Siting a house is sudden-death feng shui; if you site the house wrong—and many people do—it's wrong for a long time. Karla Greer, who has devoted her thirty-year career at the firm to working on many of the homes in this book, is especially eloquent on the risks and rewards of siting.

"We look comprehensively at the landscape," Greer says, "asking questions about how clients will use the house, how they will use the land, and how the house can assist in their appreciation and enjoyment of the place. We'll start with a passive response, what the summer and winter winds do, where the window and door openings should be, and, not least, what sort of views we have. Then we can go into active systems, whether they want photovoltaics—in other words, how far off the grid they're comfortable being."

Conducting sunlight simulations during the design process and determining the main directions of the summer and winter winds vis-à-vis the major openings help determine which way a house "faces." Some of the houses on the pages that follow—particularly those constructed as "villages" or as a series of pavilions (p. 246)—face in multiple directions and offer a multitude of seats in the landscape from which many different views are possible.

"The land itself has a big part in the dialogue," Greer says. "Sometimes we'll go to a site, and the site just *tells us* what it is that we should

House of Courts, San Antonio, Texas (1997). This lush private
courtyard offers a welcome respite from the urban setting.

do—the right piece of land can speak that clearly. Sometimes I think that cozying in, with our backs to a hill, touches some really old, primal part of us. We feel protected. And obviously, in an urban setting, it's important to choose your views and the major openings, so that you can edit out the neighbors."

Very soon after founding the firm in 1984, Lake and Flato began designing houses for clients with lots of outdoor space: specifically, with screened-in porches and huge dogtrots between pavilion-like structures dedicated to various activities. Each house was a sort of village, turned outward, toward the out-of-doors. It doesn't sound radical now, and in fact many of the houses in this volume are examples of such structures, but at the time it was a considered a huge leap backwards and a nigh-on suicidal practice for architects in Texas, the land of energy-hog air conditioning.

Twenty-two years ago, when his firm was six years old, Flato said to me: "Why air conditioning? What's wrong with the breeze? If you site the thing well to the prevailing wind, which people in Texas did for decades before air conditioning, you don't have much of a problem."

Flato, Lake, and their coterie began their professional lives with this thinking. At the time, there was no official or unofficial rating system in the United States for the energy efficiency of a building's "envelope." That was

decades off, in fact. Even the notion of an energy envelope for a building didn't yet exist. The only people who were really thinking about that were at NASA, and they only thought about it because space was a supremely hostile environment for space capsules and thus for astronauts.

There's a second, arguably less apparent but important, trend reflected in these pages. That trend is our own loss of fear about returning to the out-of-doors.

We could be forgiven for thinking that that would be a simple thing: to walk, to sit, to eat, to live outside. After all, everybody loves a great outdoor space. But, for *living*, we've been conditioned by our own rampant air conditioning—cold and hot—to fear the vagaries of the great outdoors. There's an unspoken code in America that everything must be constant. The message in these houses is that the inconstancy of the out-of-doors is exactly what makes it so enjoyable.

Looked at closely, this collection of homes allows us to track the increasing courage of this firm's clients to trust these architects and make the move outside. The corollary is that, when one trusts these architects, they will use the placement and the construction of a home to harness the out-of-doors itself. This can be as simple as installing a great overhang to provide shade, adding a pergola over a walkway, or siting a house on the bias to catch a breeze off a pond. Literally every house on every page of this book does some version of this.

Two homes stand out for what I'll call client courage and exquisite interplay of design and siting. I've been, with Flato, to one of them: the simple, beautifully radical Hill Country Jacal (p. 17). The Jacal is a second home, a country house for a city couple in a remote area on the Bear Creek, about an hour west of San Antonio. This couple came to the firm some years back, having just bought that piece of land. They didn't have much money for a house, but beyond that, they had the notion that it was possible to have a house that was off the grid. One hundred percent off the grid.

"This really developed in a very basic way from settler architecture," explains Flato as we step down the driveway to the Jacal. "You come to the country. It's your grubstake. What would you do? What's the first thing that anybody would have built for shelter? You'd dig into the hill and build a wall, and put some sort of shed roof over it. Well, we did that. The advantage of this roof is that it collects the rainwater, which is used for the shower and the toilet. But that's pretty much it."

The Jacal is basically a generous moon-shaped screened porch with no house behind it. Even in the hottest Hill Country summers, it's cooled by the creek. The stone wall, dug into the grade a foot or two, is the house. The wall curves gently with its concave side facing the water. The kitchen, storage, and sleeping nooks are masterfully fitted into it, much as the living and storage areas would be built inside the

Lasater Residence, Fort Worth, Texas (1994). Its "outdoor entrance hall" erases the line between indoors and out.

Hill Country Jacal, Pipe Creek, Texas
(1997), an off-the-grid retreat.

hull of a schooner. The master bed is out in the far southern corner of the screened-in "living room," with a view of the gold fingers of the sandbars in the winding creek just down the hill. In a stone nook on the left side of the wall is a bunk bed for the couple's two daughters. This is a sweet pioneer abode: Laura Ingalls Wilder in Texas, circa 1835. All that's missing from the picture is an Appaloosa with one rein wrapped around a post under the shed, his right rear foot cocked up on the edge of his hoof.

The second house that embraces the outdoors and shows great client courage is the reconditioned factory-turned-ranch-house in Kyle, Texas (pp. 2, 3). It's one thing for a single, tight family to dig into the hillside, as the owners of the Jacal did; it's quite another thing to dismantle a 40' x 180' x 20' Alamo Cement Plant shed, chop it into pieces, and have it reassembled as three giant structures, two of which are screened and/or semi-covered—and then to live in those structures. Within the main "living" shed are isolated, covered modules for kitchen and bath, but this house cleaves quite closely to the idea of total outdoor living.

There's a third important aspect to both of these high-risk homes, evinced earlier—one that is crucial to understanding what has happened to Lake|Flato in the thirty years since its founding and to where it is headed. Both houses are what can only be described as *hyperlocal*—which is not a word, but which gets at the idea. Lake and Flato had been driving by, and admiring, the Alamo Cement Plant for years. When they learned it was scheduled for demolition, and the right risk-friendly client came along, they sold it to him *as his house*. In the Jacal's case, the hyperlocality lies in the deep vernacular quoting of the sodbuster lean-to. That design was considered outré, temporary, poor-man's housing by the nineteenth-century settlers themselves. Here it's been turned into a stage for pure, funky, camping-out joy by the river. In terms of a living structure in Texas, you'd be hard-pressed to get any more "local" than that.

Lake and Flato began their professional lives thinking this way—the Jacal was quite an early commission—and they never stopped. The relentless use of local metaphors extends to their corporate and commercial work: the San Antonio Spurs stadium, a.k.a. the AT&T Center, is basically a giant feed barn, with huge silos at each corner that contain the stairwells, clad in corrugated steel. The wildly popular stadium, which also hosts San Antonio's famous annual rodeo, is an example of how Lake|Flato have made hyperlocality scalable. They can take an enormous cement factory shed, chop it like sushi chefs, and bring it down to a ranch as a family residence, or they can take a shit-kicking Texas feed barn, blow it up like a pool float, and give seats to 18,000 for an NBA playoff game.

In residential terms, this scalability is most apparent in the development of the Porch House (pp. 58–71), under the aegis of founding firm member Bill Aylor. Aylor, the lead architect for the firm in the construction of Cross Timbers Ranch (pp. 28–39)—an extremely high-end bespoke house—has also taken the lead on the Porch House iteration of home architecture. With a Porch House, it's possible for a client to select any number of modules—in effect, prefabricated rooms or pavilions—that can be assembled according to the client's wishes. This is a fine example of the firm's ability to combine two basically contradictory ideas: the idea of custom architecture and the idea of prefabrication.

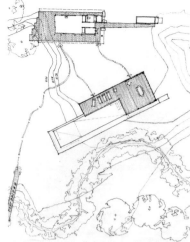

Site/floor plan.

Broadford Farm Pavilion, Hailey, Idaho (2003).
Sliding doors open the corner of the pavilion
fully to the outdoors.

As we might imagine with a firm whose designs are rooted in simplicity, the choice of materials and the details of the structures play a large role in the earliest phases of a project. Partner Brian Korte arrived at a particularly elegant marriage of form, economy, and craft in his Broadford Farm Pavilion. The viewer's eye is drawn, first, to the openness and simplicity of the structure. It has a shed roof; an "open" side toward the pool and the mountains with a glass front that encompasses the view; and the kitchen/bar, dressing room, and bath form the building's back. The rafters are of reclaimed Douglas fir, native to Idaho.

But let's draw the reader's eye to the thinking and the craft that went into the structural steel: the columns that carry the "box" of the four horizontal steel beams that support the clerestory. It's as if the little house has a steel belt around its middle. The columns then work up to support the "flitch" rafters, which are made from two pieces of reclaimed Douglas fir bolted to a steel spine running between them. The frame is a very light, almost invisible box of steel, like the frame of a jet plane, upon which the whole pavilion hangs.

"Detail begins with how a building comes out of the ground, how the different materials meet, and what happens where they meet," Korte says. "The gist of this pavilion is that the horizontal 'beams' are actually two steel C-channels fitted back to back, with a wooden beam between them providing a thermal break, but also giving us a piece of wood from which we could hang the sliding doors and to which we could attach the windows above. The doors

are straight-grain Douglas fir, custom-made. The reason the steel columns are twelve inches out from the walls was to put the structure outside the frame of the building—it's in an earthquake zone—but that does double duty, in that it allows for bigger runs of glass and a better view. It's like a modern pole-barn."

Not unexpectedly, the Idaho client was tremendously happy with the natural ease and soundness of the design. A few years after he had it built, he decided to sell the ranch, but he wrote an unusual precondition into the sale: the Pool Pavilion was uprooted and moved lock, stock, and barrel down the road to overlook the pool on his new ranch. That doesn't happen to a lot of outbuildings when ranches trade hands.

Lucky Boy Ranch, Mason, Texas (2004). Shady outdoor rooms, like this generous two-story porch, are hallmarks of Lake|Flato's work.

Homes take many forms. We could say that the taproots of Lake|Flato's work drive deep into the sediments of history—and not just the immediate, human history of Texas, although the firm does do that very well because it is from, and of, the state. As they pore over every project, these architects also drive back into the prehistory of the rock and the wood as the region was washed over by the seas. Like a group of paleontologists, they take their vocabulary of materials, and the language for what to do with those materials, from this deep, old way of looking at the world. It's a rare thing to imagine a piece of architecture not so much as a manufactured structure that one brings to a place, but rather as a structure that comes *from* a place. There's a vast difference in the world of architecture between those two propositions.

This is why the homes in this book look like they grew up where they are. It's also the reason why this book is organized on the principles and demands of geography, topography, and climate. The point of Lake|Flato's work is that, as the earth takes many forms, so do our ways of living upon it. The chapters that follow are not ordered by the "type" of architecture—there is no "type" here, anyway—but rather by the elements: the land, the wind, the water, and the sun. These are the larger forces that work on each of us, and they are the forces that these homes are made to fit.

There's something strong, and restful, and right about shelter that keeps to the earth's order of things. It's what a home should do.

House of Light, Santa Fe, New Mexico (1996). Sunlight is a critical component of Lake|Flato's environmental design process.

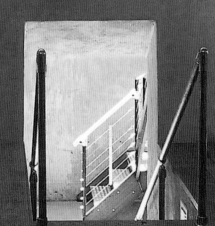

BRUSHLAND

For early Texas settlers, the territory's vast brushlands presented formidable challenges. These scruffy expanses were not easy to farm or to inhabit. However, these lands grew in value, initially as hardscrabble ranches; then for the wealth below the surface; and eventually for their intrinsic, sublime beauty.

Lake|Flato Architects capture the practicality of the ranches, the ability to use the earth, and the grandeur of wide-open spaces. In these hot lands with few trees, shade and breezes provide welcome relief. Ranchers have long employed practical architecture that made common sense, simple buildings with big porches oriented to take advantage of the prevailing Texas summer winds from the southeast. Lake|Flato builds on these vernacular precedents as well as on the welding skills and the materials-recycling tradition of the oil fields. Its brushland ranches feature large porches to provide ample shade and capture breezes. Buildings are arranged around open courtyards to further funnel winds. The architects situate the barns in a similar fashion, as horses also enjoy shade and a good breeze.

Lake|Flato ranches build on the landscape of the past to create contemporary spaces. For instance, for the Cross Timbers Ranch, the design retained both natural (a mott of oak trees) and cultural (a water tank) features, incorporating them into four pavilions using an innovative closed-loop geothermal heating and cooling system.

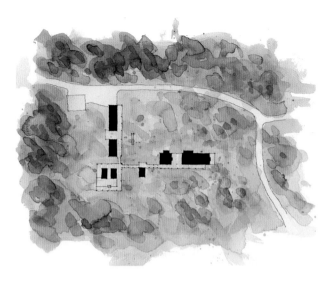

CROSS TIMBERS RANCH
TEXAS

Cross Timbers is a ranch house and family retreat located in the expansive landscape of north Texas. The ranch consists of four separate pavilions nestled in a grove of oak trees dividing a pasture from a river valley, with each structure serving a specific function. A central living room acts as the public pavilion of the compound, while the master bedroom, guest bedrooms, and wine cellar/overlook complete the courtyard. Breaking up the program in this way allows the compound to be used comfortably by either large groups or a single family.

The structures, built of local indigenous materials such as sinker cypress, stone, weathered steel pipe, and galvanized metal panels, find their formal inspiration in the modest vernacular ranch buildings, barns, and sheds of the region. Shady porches connect the four pavilions and frame a series of courtyards anchored by existing oak trees. These outdoor rooms capture the prevailing breezes and help cool the adjacent interior spaces. The compound uses an innovative 100-percent closed-loop geothermal system for its heating and cooling, for a substantial energy savings.

Overall, the project is defined by its modest scale, simple detailing, and seamless integration into the landscape.

The cellar is partially buried in the earth so that its
elevated roof becomes a raised vantage point, while its
concrete recesses take advantage of the earth's cooling
for wine storage. The concrete ceiling, formed from
recycled oil barrels, pays homage to the land's history.

The structures are finished to appear much like the modest structures that are found on the surrounding ranch—steel pipe fencing, wood-clad barns, corrugated metal shade structures, etc.

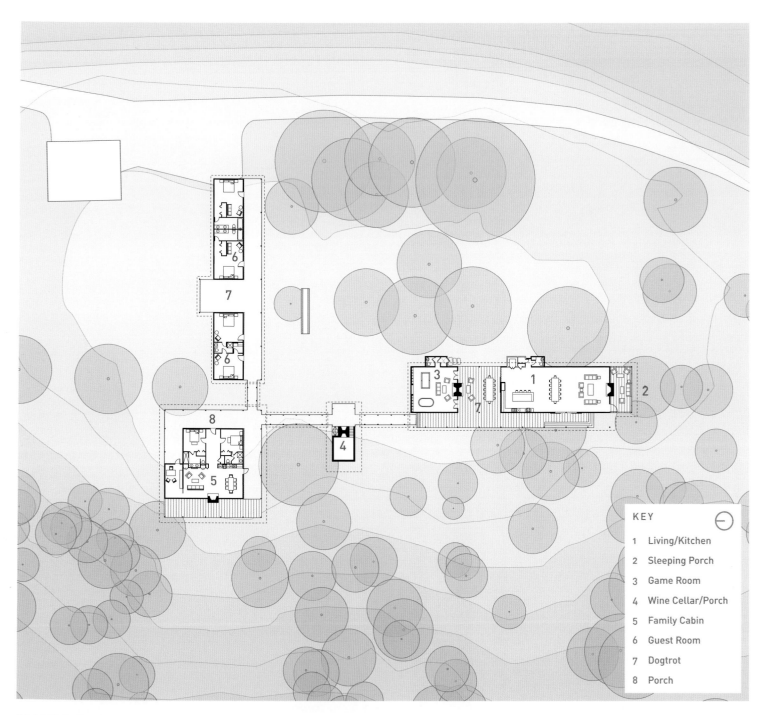

KEY

⊖

1   Living/Kitchen

2   Sleeping Porch

3   Game Room

4   Wine Cellar/Porch

5   Family Cabin

6   Guest Room

7   Dogtrot

8   Porch

The slatted screened porch enjoys dappled light patterns as the sun moves around the house.

Handcrafted steel details define the character of the interior spaces.

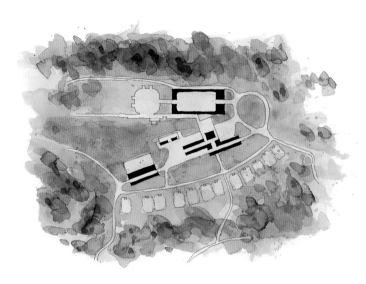

CUTTING HORSE RANCH
TEXAS

Located on rolling rangeland west of Fort Worth, Cutting Horse Ranch was designed to be one of the premiere equine facilities in the country, providing all necessary amenities for the care, training, and breeding of competition cutting horses.

Despite the variety of scales and purposes, the steel-framed structures of the complex are tied together by a common palette of materials and a familiar language of forms that recall the simple agricultural and ranch buildings that dot the north Texas landscape. Pipe columns and trusses with plate connectors are used consistently to unite both the humble service structures and the centerpiece of the project, a 45,000-square-foot arena. The arena is protected from the harsh Texas sun and cold winter winds by weathered, perforated metal–paneled walls that also allow for cross-ventilation and abundant natural light. Additional structures include a ranch office, staff dining hall, tack room, and veterinary and wash facilities, as well as a training barn, a mare barn, and a state-of-the-art hydrotherapy barn with an equine therapy pool. The entire complex, with its form, materials, and orientation all responding to environmental conditions, is a comfortable place for both man and horse, even during a hot Texas summer.

Continuous ridge vents in all of the barns ensures a cool experience even in the hottest Texas summers.

Perforated metal walls maximize light and ventilation while keeping strong winds and rain at bay.

Hydrotherapy barn.

50

Water off the roofs is
collected and used
for irrigation in the
adjacent courtyard.

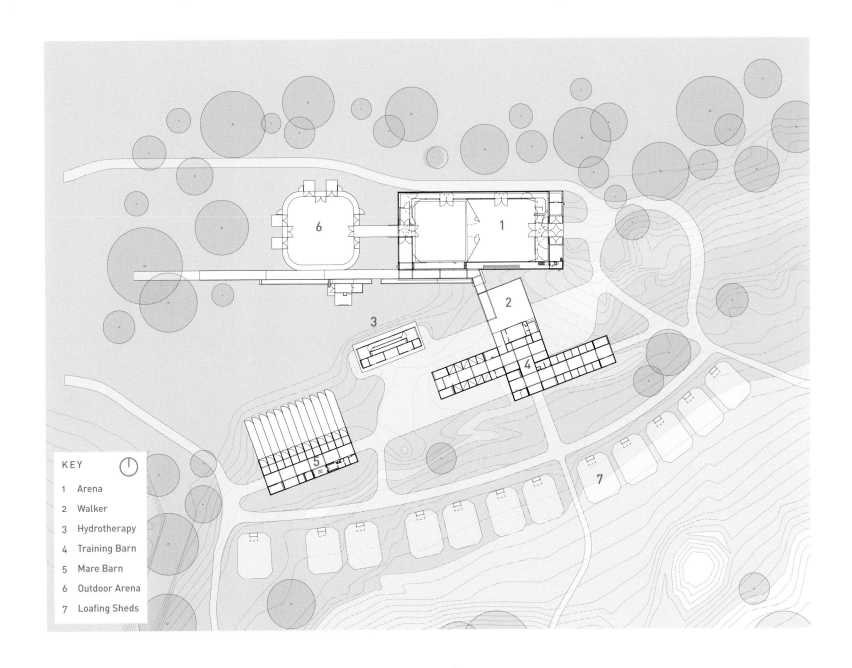

KEY

1 Arena
2 Walker
3 Hydrotherapy
4 Training Barn
5 Mare Barn
6 Outdoor Arena
7 Loafing Sheds

The arena, with its perforated metal skin, has great natural light and ventilation.

The rusted steel connections of the barns leverage the local welding tradition.

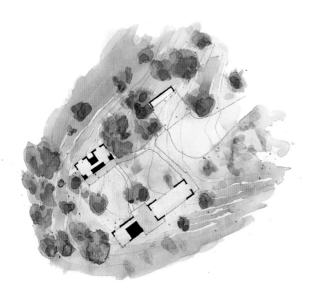

PORCH HOUSE
TEXAS

Inspired by the challenges of working in remote locations, the Lake|Flato Porch House presents a new way of thinking, designing, and building for our residential clients. Based on a library of factory-constructed, modular living and sleeping rooms, the Porch House concept enables a design-conscious owner to have a custom-built, site-specific, LEED-certified Lake|Flato house with predictable outcomes in terms of quality, time, and cost. Porches and other outdoor areas, built on-site, serve as connecting tissue to create exciting outdoor spaces and ensure that each house is particular to its place.

The first "prototype," the Miller Porch House, located on a ranch in Central Texas, was built as a weekend house for friends and family that would celebrate the outdoors. The rooms, a master bedroom connected to the living area via a "dog run" breezeway and separate guest bedrooms and carport, are arranged to take advantage of the expansive views while creating a protected courtyard within the compound.

The one-room-wide configuration with an east-west axis and generous overhangs maximizes daytime lighting and views while keeping the sun at bay. Generous ten-foot-tall windows and doors, porches, and breezeways allow the rooms to take advantage of the cool coastal breezes during pleasant times of the year.

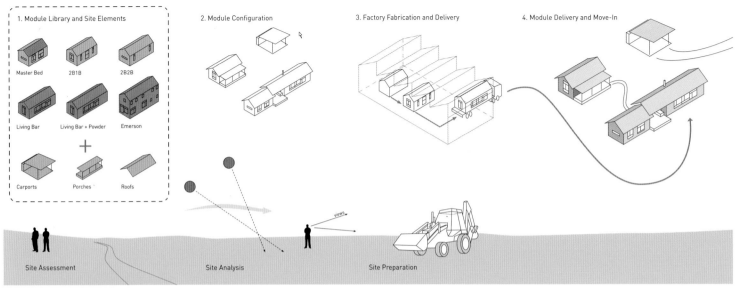

1. Module Library and Site Elements

Master Bed   2B1B   2B2B

Living Bar   Living Bar + Powder   Emerson

+

Carports   Porches   Roofs

2. Module Configuration

3. Factory Fabrication and Delivery

4. Module Delivery and Move-In

views

Site Assessment   Site Analysis   Site Preparation

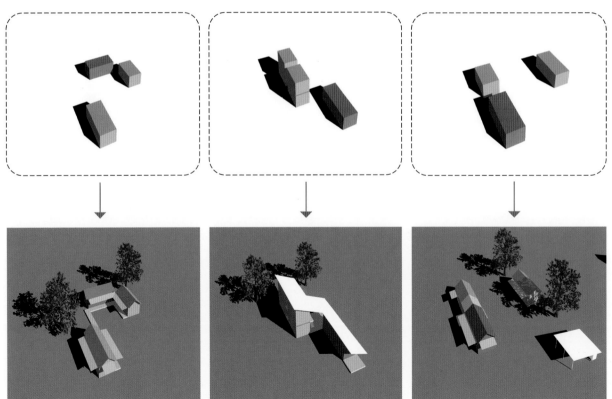

FLEXIBLE MODULES

The factory-built rooms are arranged on the site to take advantage of views, breezes, solar orientation, and outdoor spaces. The custom-designed site-built "porch elements," such as breezeways, porches, overhangs, and carports, are the "connecting tissue" that hold the rooms together while allowing the overall design to adapt to the unique characteristics of the site, the weather, and the client's program.

ROOMS

Factory-constructed rooms, where the finishes and "mechanical systems" are installed in a controlled environment, allow for a consistently high-quality product as well as an energy-efficient construction process. The variety of living and sleeping rooms with their wide range of finishes, combined with the myriad ways of organizing them, provides our clients a great deal of flexibility in assembling their ultimate Porch House.

 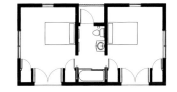 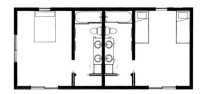

Bedrooms

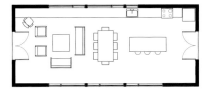 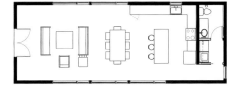

Living areas

 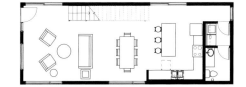

Two-story units

SUSTAINABILITY

The modular design process, in which rooms are constructed in multiples, has allowed Lake|Flato to test and refine its product with the ultimate goal of simplicity, beauty, and sustainability. Combined with the site-built porch elements, the Porch House is designed to use much less energy than a typical house and earn LEED certification. With the addition of photovoltaic solar panels—a Porch House design option— clients can choose to have a net-zero energy consumption house.

Factory-constructed modules

Delivery.

KEY

1. Carport
2. Two Bed, One Bath Guest House
3. Master Bedroom
4. Living Bar
5. Porch

The overall composition of the house with its room-to-room circulation on the porches maximizes the connection to the outdoors while achieving energy efficiency.

The exterior materials of the house were selected for low maintenance: corrugated galvanized metal on the exterior walls that are exposed to the elements, with local cedar siding on the protected porches.

A movable slatted cedar wall can be pulled to one side to block harsh winds.

DESERT

Each landscape poses specific constraints on an architect. Charles Eames observed that "design depends largely on constraints." But no landscape presents as many constraints as a desert: a tough environment, characterized by low precipitation and, as a result, few plants.

Lake|Flato's desert houses echo Frank Lloyd Wright's organic approach to architecture, as exemplified by Taliesin West. As Wright created a refuge at Taliesin from the harsh conditions of the Arizona Sonoran Desert, so does Lake|Flato by building pleasant, shady oases. The architects accomplish this through the use of courtyards, massive walls, and deep-set windows. Their courtyard houses filter light, edit views of the surrounding desert, use native plants, and employ water strategically. Lake|Flato employs light throughout the day and through the seasons to connect the indoors with the outdoors. Natural light bounces off the walls and floors with shadows that change with the angle of the sun dancing through the rooms.

The Brown Residence in Arizona provides an example. The way the horizontal house fits among the plants and boulders of the landscape presents clear similarities with Taliesin. The architects sited the Brown Residence to protect the tall, columnar saguaro cacti, green-stemmed palo verde trees, and other Sonoran plants. The residence exhibits organic architecture in the Wright sense, but to an even greater degree it illustrates the "appropriate architecture" of Lake|Flato.

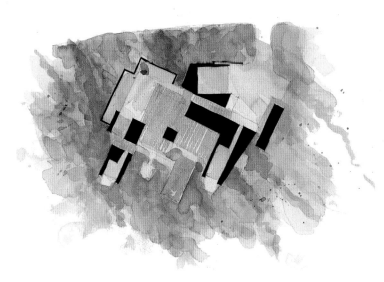

BROWN RESIDENCE
SCOTTSDALE, ARIZONA

Despite being amongst other houses, the Brown Residence capitalizes on the stunning views of the adjacent Sonoran Desert landscape. The organization of open steel and glass living spaces and solid stucco bedroom volumes strategically blocks the views of neighboring houses while creating outdoor rooms and a seamless connection to the desert.

While the residence appears modest and unassuming from the street, it steps down with the slope of the site and creates increasingly generous interior spaces. An open breezeway between the house's two building volumes serves as the main entrance and immediately provides views of both the private courtyard and the surrounding desert. Oversized pivot doors and large expanses of glass allow abundant light and the seasonally temperate desert climate to fill the interior spaces. Broad overhangs shade the glass-enclosed living spaces from the harsh desert sun.

Cast-in-place concrete garden walls, native stone paving, and indigenous landscaping define this main courtyard as well as several other smaller courts tucked in between buildings. Ground concrete continues inside as the predominant floor material while stained mesquite paneling and flooring provide warmth throughout the house. A simple steel-clad swimming pool adjacent to the family room provides respite from the desert heat.

Simple stucco forms ground the house to the site and contrast with the more voluminous steel and glass living area that floats within the sheltered courtyards.

Concrete and steel garden walls define
outdoor spaces that unite the indoors
with the out.

A floating mesquite wall in the dining pavilion creates closure
while still maintaining a strong connection to the outdoors.

Rusted steel bars filter the bright sun.

KEY   🕐

1   Entry

2   Dining/Living Room

3   Kitchen

4   Master

5   Guest

6   Sunken Courtyard

7   Pool

8   Garage

The main living spaces spill out into the rugged desert courtyards.

DESERT HOUSE

SANTA FE, NEW MEXICO

The heavy stucco walls of this rustic modern hacienda reach out into the land, holding back earth, to create a succession of courtyards, an oasis of calm—a refuge. Interior and exterior spaces were designed to accommodate the client's art collection while providing a practical shelter in this harsh desert climate.

A bridge building spans two long walls at the entry to create a portal leading to the hidden entry court. A low entry gallery compresses space before ramping down to the main living space, a long shed open at both ends with generous portales providing shade from the sun. This tube of light, shuttered from direct sunlight, is the center of the house for both art and living. Exposed concrete walls retain the earth and the light steel roof "hovers" above to capture southern light and heat. At the end of the room is the kitchen, which opens to a sunrise portal with mountain views and a path leading to the partially buried guest-room wing.

The quiet volumes of light allow art to reside and views to be present, yet buffered. Outside, the landscape is bounded by walls that create verdant garden rooms, in contrast to the desert horizon. These features were all intended to create a house that is a comfortable refuge in a challenging yet beautiful environment.

Located north of Santa Fe in desert terrain, this house is a modern interpretation of a hacienda.

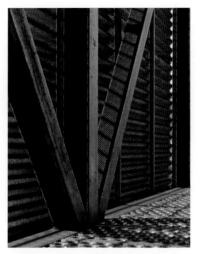

Courtyards were formed by the installation of low buildings lying east-west, linked by outdoor-oriented loggias and porches.

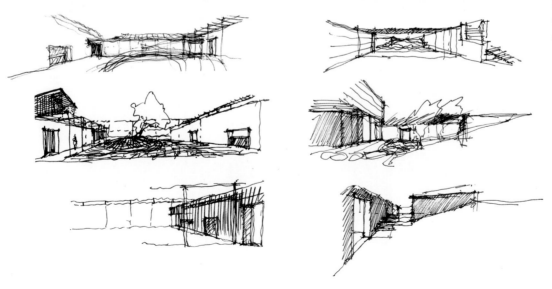

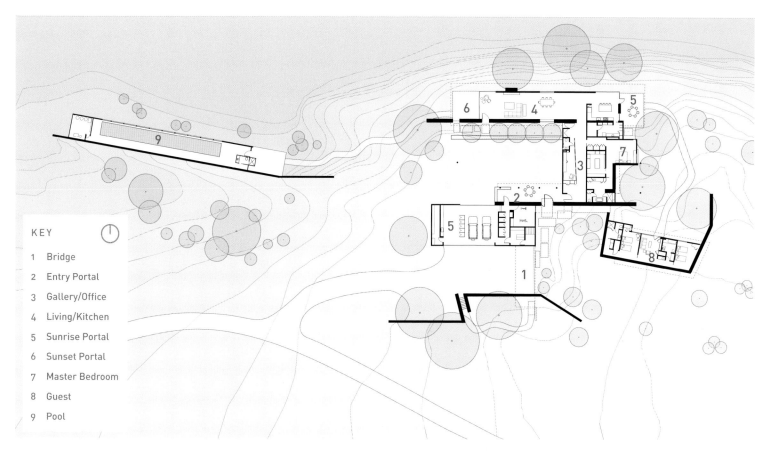

KEY   ①

1   Bridge

2   Entry Portal

3   Gallery/Office

4   Living/Kitchen

5   Sunrise Portal

6   Sunset Portal

7   Master Bedroom

8   Guest

9   Pool

An interior pool that doubles as a gallery.

Low entry gallery contrasts with the voluminous
living area beyond.

The thick parallel walls of the living area accommodate art while maintaining a connection with the outdoors.

Smaller, more intimate bedrooms are a nice counterpoint to the adjacent expansive courtyards.

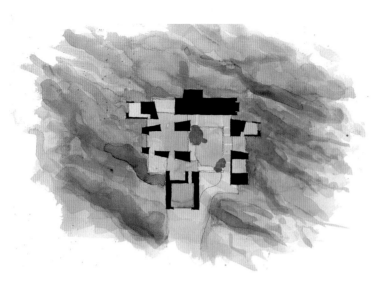

DUNNING RESIDENCE
SANTA FE, NEW MEXICO

Santa Fe retains a stylistic consistency almost unique among American cities. In designing the Dunning Residence, Lake|Flato decided that developing a new take on the traditional Spanish Pueblo Revival style was a critical first step in creating a modern house that would meet the needs of its contemporary clients.

The Dunning Residence is located on an open hillside northwest of Santa Fe. The site provides tremendous views of the high desert, distant mountain peaks, and the faint lights of Los Alamos. Individual building volumes and the windows located within those masses are organized to frame specific views while at the same time sheltering the occupants from the intense New Mexico sun.

The compound consists of six simple stucco volumes connected by both open and enclosed porches. These portales frame a central courtyard that acts as a protected oasis within the harsh desert. The stucco-clad rooms step up the grade of the hill, culminating in the large main living space that anchors the compound. Deeply inset punched windows provide views from the interiors while sheltering the occupants from the intensity of the direct sun. Daylight is allowed to seep in at specific locations, making the house an inhabitable sundial that tracks the passage of time and the seasons.

A simple regional palette of building materials and finishes reflects the colors and textures of the desert landscape.

The shading and editing nature of the minimalist sculpture of Donald Judd helped influence the design of the house.

Service elements are
concealed by thick walls
that frame views and
admit glare-free light.

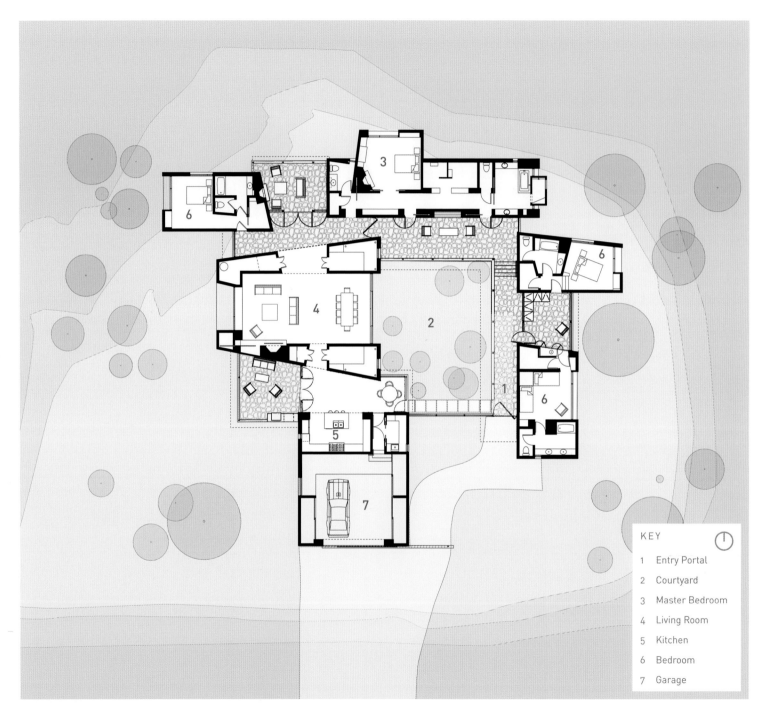

KEY

1   Entry Portal

2   Courtyard

3   Master Bedroom

4   Living Room

5   Kitchen

6   Bedroom

7   Garage

HILLSIDE

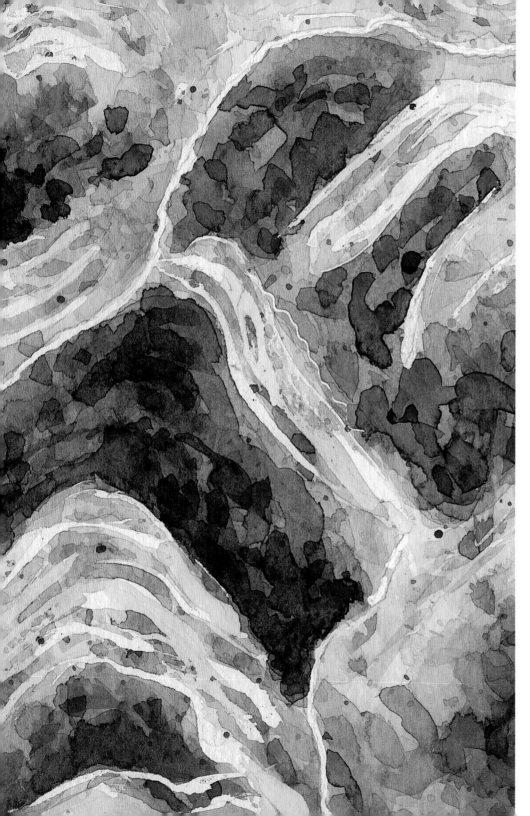

The opportunities and constraints presented by hillsides vary with site-specific circumstances. North-, south-, east-, and west-facing hills receive different amounts of sunlight and, often, precipitation. Slope orientation, then, determines the specific plants that grow and the distinct soil types that form. Accomplished architects learn to read the language of hillside landscapes to inspire and guide their designs.

Lake|Flato Architects have designed houses for the mesa hillsides of California as well as the rolling hills of Texas. They have employed stone walls and terraces, similar to the manner in which hillsides are farmed, to adapt to specific soil and slope conditions. Their hillside houses with sheltering walls and rolling panels turn potentially exposed locations into comfortable places.

In many American cities, significant natural patches remain where architects are challenged to retain aspects of remnant landscape while inserting new, inherently disruptive structures. Hillside House, with its dramatic views of downtown Austin, represents such an insertion. Lake|Flato built the house on a small footprint to minimize disruption and to take advantage of the natural sloping attributes of the site.

Lake|Flato Architects has been on the forefront of the green building design movement, which is evident in Hillside House. Both the siting (to minimize western exposures) and the use of appropriate, energy-conserving building materials contribute to a house that is both responsive and responsible.

HILLSIDE HOUSE
AUSTIN, TEXAS

Situated on a steeply sloping "pie-shaped" site with stunning views of downtown Austin is this low-profile structure, Hillside House. The challenge for the architects was to create a building that takes advantage of the distant views while also maintaining close ties to the adjacent hardscape. The house is terraced into two levels, with the main living areas and master bedroom on one level and the children's wing on a lower level. By using the roof of the children's wing as a green roof and retaining structure, and by preserving a stand of fifty-year-old live oak trees in the process, a generous at-grade courtyard was created off the living room and kitchen. The below-grade and green roof construction of the children's wing provides excellent thermal efficiency while still allowing the rooms to flow out to the pool terrace at the lowest level of the house. Massive blocks of locally quarried Texas limestone create a series of low building and landscape walls that merge the house with the site and provide a contrast to the light, airy wood pavilions.

Building orientation, shading and minimal western exposures, thermally broken window and door systems, high R-value, native wall and paving stones, high-recycled-content steel, common wood species, and minimal lighting all contribute to a regionally appropriate and energy-responsive solution.

Larger, dry-stacked walls, made from locally quarried limestone, greet the
visitor at the street and create protected courtyards for the rooms beyond.

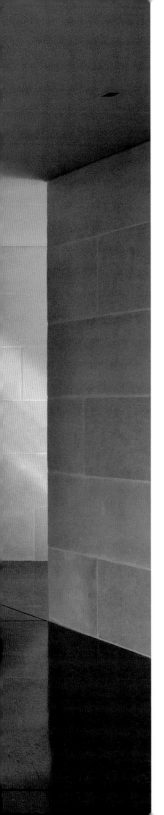

The limestone walls unite the outdoors with the interior of the house.

Expansive windows and a generous overhang afford broad views of downtown Austin.

128

Native Texas stone, used to create the
exterior, provides a contrast to the light,
airy wood pavilions.

A generous stair connects the
lower-level children's wing
with the main public rooms of
the house.

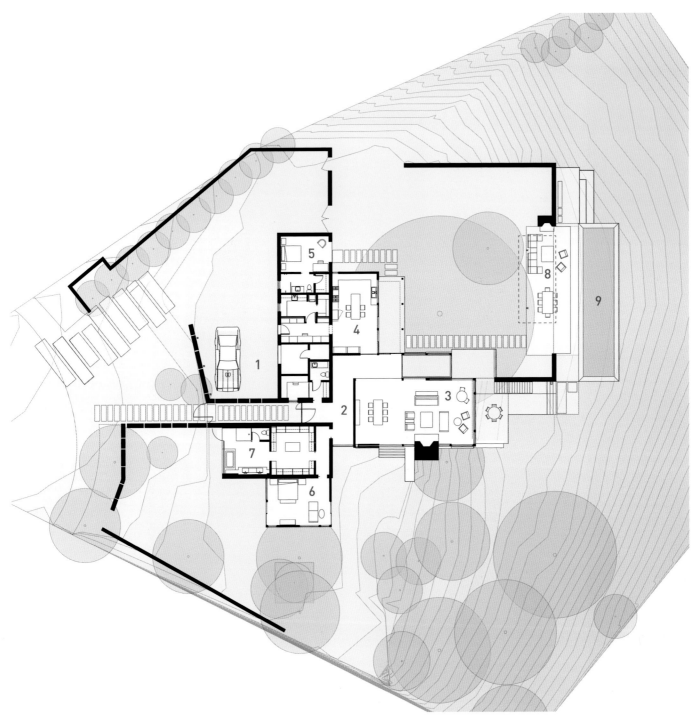

KEY

1 Carport

2 Entry

3 Living Room

4 Kitchen

5 Guest Suite

6 Master Bedroom

7 Master Bathroom

8 Terrace with children's
   wing below

9 Pool

Limestone garden walls create a private courtyard for the master bath and bedroom.

By using the roof of the children's wing as a "green roof" and retaining structure,
a generous "at-grade" courtyard was created off the living room and kitchen.

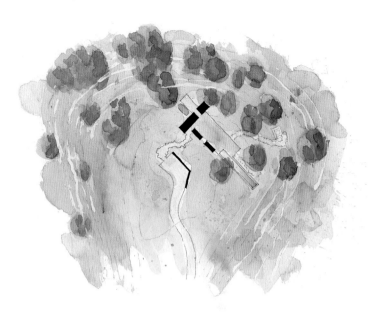

STORY POOL HOUSE
CENTER POINT, TEXAS

The missing piece at the Story Ranch was a "sunrise to sunset" outdoor family gathering place that would be set apart from the more private ranch house that was designed a number of years ago. The land is composed of a series of plateaus with expansive views of the Texas Hill Country. One plateau had served as an informal gathering spot for years, with a lonely, restored Airstream trailer and fire pit, so it was there that Lake|Flato placed the new structure.

The solution was a simple, open-air, steel and wood, outdoor living room pavilion sheltered behind thick limestone walls that house a full working kitchen, bath, and storage space. The Airstream was given its own special environment with a small private deck under a vine-covered arbor structure—all nestled in the shade of a large grouping of trees. The pool, which begins in the shade of the generous living area, extends out into the landscape like an enormous "water trough," connecting the modest shelter to the sloping hillside and distant views.

The light steel and wood roof protects the main living area from the sun, while the massive limestone walls create shelter from the wind.

The pool extends
out into the
landscape like
an enormous
water trough.

142

KEY   ⏱

1   Entry

2   Lap Pool

3   Outdoor Living

4   Fire Ring

5   Airstream

6   Arbor

The stone walls house a full working kitchen.

The airstream has it own private, shaded environment.

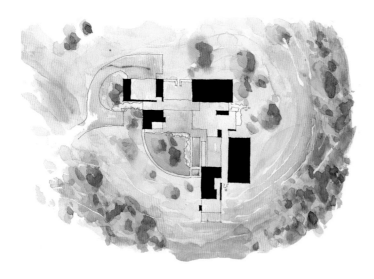

TOUCHE PASS HOUSE
CARMEL, CALIFORNIA

While known for its beautiful undulating terrain, northern California also enjoys a remarkably temperate climate throughout the year. This allows for a unique connection between indoor rooms and outdoor living areas. The Touche Pass House was designed to take advantage of this appealing climate and is organized to allow the owners—a couple and their young children— to spend as much of their day out-of-doors as inside. Inspired by the informality of local farm complexes, the house comprises several separate structures that are joined by indoor/ outdoor living spaces, creating a seamless connection between the home and the verdant landscape of rolling hills and oak groves.

The primary structure is a partially open/ partially enclosed barnlike space whose formal steel structure provides a simple frame through which to view the landscape beyond. Continuing the feeling of an informal agricultural compound, the private rooms of the house define the edges of this open living area and create smaller complementary outdoor spaces.

Throughout the house, sliding glass walls and a consistency of materials blur the distinction between inside and out. The crisp detailing, glass openings, and generous overhangs make this a uniquely family-appropriate and site-specific house. Dry-stack stonework and weathered metal roof planes combine to make a structure that is very much at home in this gentle landscape.

146

Reminiscent of a farm compound, the house creates a series of outdoor living areas.

KEY

1 Entry

2 Outdoor Living Room

3 Entry Hall

4 Living Room/Kitchen

5 Family

6 Garden

7 Garage

8 Bedroom Suite

9 Master Bedroom

10 Lap Pool

11 Guest

A large pivoting gate opens
on to an outdoor entry hall.

The heart of the house is the vine-covered outdoor living area.

The kitchen is sandwiched between the indoor and outdoor living areas.

An indoor/outdoor gallery with large sliding doors connects the bedroom wing with the main living area.

MOUNTAIN

Mountains rise up from their surroundings creating various ecologies with environments that are much wetter and colder than the surrounding lowlands. Many cultures attach myths and legends to mountain peaks. Mountains represent the deep structure of our planet. They capture water and bring life to the lands below their heights. They stand as representations of geologic time. Mountains humble us, putting our aspirations and existence into perspective.

Lake|Flato Architects have created poetic houses across the mountains of the American West in Colorado, Idaho, Montana, and Nevada. They design spaces that can adjust through the seasons, doubling as open porches during the summers and enclosed rooms during the winters. The houses are sited to take advantage of dramatic mountain vistas.

As one example, LC Ranch in Three Forks, Montana, is situated in an especially spectacular mountainous environment with extreme weather conditions. The ranch is designed to be inhabited in all seasons. Lake|Flato drew on the vernacular home and barn building traditions of the region. For instance, the architects updated the use of sod in constructing an earthen roof over the bedrooms to cool the rooms in the summer and warm them through the winter. The living spaces also have timber roofs and large sliding doors that evoke elements of Montana barns.

LC RANCH
THREE FORKS, MONTANA

The state of Montana possesses some of the most dramatic landscapes in the continental United States, as well as some of the most extreme weather conditions. The LC Ranch was designed in response to these climatic extremes, so that its owners could enjoy the surrounding countryside regardless of the season. The house sits in the transition between rolling hills covered with native short grasses and the riparian valley of the Gallatin River. A spring-fed pond flows into a narrow creek that is parallel to the house, seen and heard from every room.

In building the house, the architects found inspiration in two regional building types—the simple gabled barn and the earthen sodbuster homes of the early settlers. The public living, dining, and kitchen spaces are collected in a long gabled space that presents a strong contrast to the private spaces. To take advantage of the site's more temperate summer climate, the main barnlike living space can open to the site with a series of large sliding doors that wrap around the building. When open, the space becomes a light-filled screened pavilion overlooking the valley and creeks below. During the winter, the space can be closed down using large rolling insulated panels to protect the glazing and provide shelter from the harsh Montana winter. In contrast, the private bedrooms nestle under a sod roof keeping them cool in the summer and warm in the winter.

The public areas are collected
under one big barnlike roof.

A light steel frame gives the big roof an airy quality.

The poured-in-place concrete retaining walls are exposed throughout. A modern sodbuster, the house has a palette of simple materials—concrete, steel, and wood—that are taken from common buildings in the region.

The living room wing can open and close
to the site with a series of sliding doors
that wrap the building. In the summer,
glass doors disappear into pockets and
are replaced by screen doors, allowing
a seamless connection to the outdoors;
in the winter, the glass doors seal up the
space, allowing broad views, or a layer of
solid insulated doors can be used to close
up the building, reducing the glass area,
to better maintain thermal control.

This familiar barn form is the dominant element, with porches bracketing the living space and with the support spaces (laundry, mechanical, and mud room) tucked below sod roofs. The private sleeping quarters are also below a sod roof with an outdoor loggia facing southwest, linking the private wing to the public.

The private spaces under the sod roof offer a "cavelike" experience, in contrast with that of the barnlike public areas.

BARTLIT RESIDENCE
CASTLE PINES, COLORADO

The Rocky Mountain Front Range is a rugged and wild landscape where the weather is dominant. The goal in building the Bartlit Residence was to "create a seamless connection to the outdoors" while minimizing the impact of the house upon the site.

The house is anchored to the site with long stone walls that terminate in granite boulders, and a portion of it nestles below a sod roof. The public rooms are lightweight pavilions that perch on the cliff edge, in contrast to the bedrooms, which burrow into the hillside and are covered with a sod roof featuring native grasses. In addition to providing thermal benefits, the nestling of the house into the downward slope also acts to reduce its

apparent mass. Growing organically from the bedrock of the site, the house reveals itself to be a composition of anchoring walls and floors of native granite boulders with lightweight roofs of copper that meld with the subtle bronze colors of the native hillside. Naturally finished white oak, painted steel, and weathered copper complete the palette of materials.

While the plan may appear haphazard, it in fact represents a choreographed sequence of spaces and views designed to capture the unique characteristics of the home's dramatic site. A series of courtyards and interior atriums maintains a foreground intimacy that contrasts with the expansive presence of the distant mountains and wild weather, balancing shelter and openness.

Stoneclad, sod-roofed bedrooms lock the house into the mountainside and help shelter it in both winter and summer.

Steel, glass, and copper public pavilions take advantage of the heroic views while contrasting with the earthen private areas.

KEY

1 Entry
2 Gallery
3 Living Room
4 Kitchen/Family
5 Atrium
6 Bedroom
7 Garage
8 Fitness

The stone walls extend into the house and create intimate courtyards that celebrate the rugged hillside.

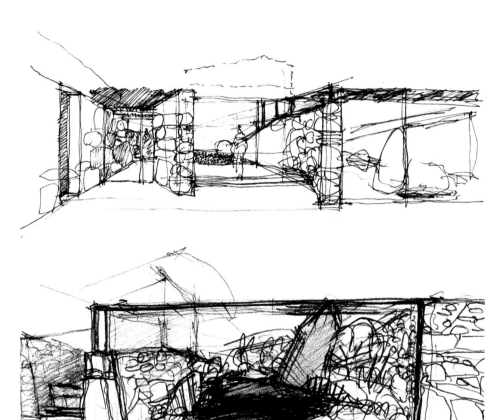

The pathway to the eastern entrance is marked by boulders and walls of granite and stone,
which extend into the interior. The walls merge with the land and lock the house into the hillside.

Large boulders embrace the living room area.

Colorado sandstone floors and oak
cabinets were used throughout the house.

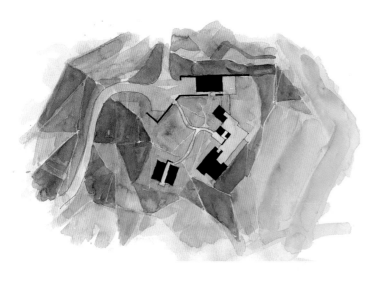

LAKE TAHOE RESIDENCE
LAKE TAHOE, NEVADA

Before it became known for its natural beauty, the region around the Sierra Nevada was known for its gold and silver deposits. The historic mines of this region provided the formal starting point for the design of this vacation home located near Lake Tahoe. The use of exposed concrete, weathered wood, and protruding bays of weathered steel create a rugged exterior that is appropriate given the site's history and harsh winter climate. It also provides a foil to the warm, natural materials that define the interior spaces.

The house is divided into three separate buildings that loosely define an informal courtyard that allowed for the preservation of the site's numerous existing trees. The simple roofs of these buildings recall the slopes of the mountains beyond.

One entire side of the large living/dining room is glazed and oriented to collect both warm winter sun and cool summer breezes. Located off of this large interior volume is a partially enclosed inglenook reading area. This strategy of contrasting small shiplike bunk spaces and built-in storage niches with larger interior volumes pervades the design. The bedrooms feature built-in bunks and banquettes that, when fully occupied, can accommodate up to twenty-four overnight guests. The detached guesthouse can serve as a stand-alone house when the complex is occupied by larger groups of visitors.

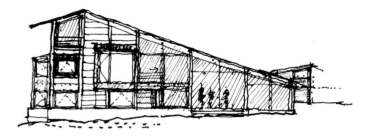

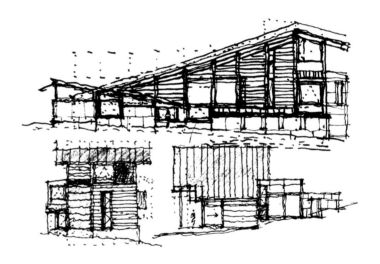

The simple shed forms of the historic mines of the region inspired the "camp" design; the residence can accommodate twenty-four overnight guests.

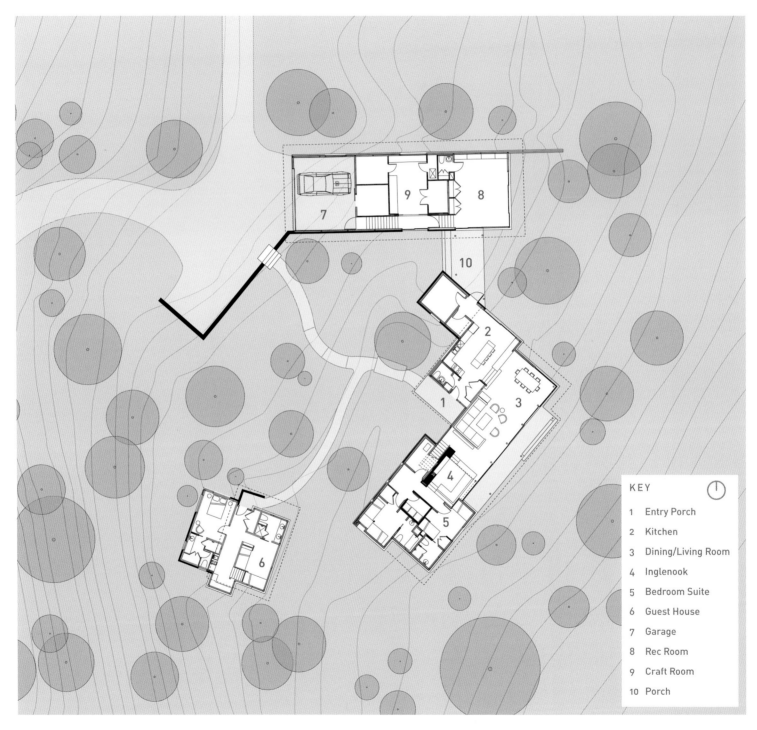

KEY

1   Entry Porch

2   Kitchen

3   Dining/Living Room

4   Inglenook

5   Bedroom Suite

6   Guest House

7   Garage

8   Rec Room

9   Craft Room

10 Porch

The home economizes on space with cabinetry under all the kitchen counters and storage under the stairs.

Small bedrooms feature bunk beds built into compact niches to accommodate children.

A muted palette of materials, including weathered wood,
exposed concrete, and Cor-Ten steel, allows the buildings
to blend into their surroundings.

CITY

The balance between nature and culture tilts toward the latter in urban places. Still, as our planet grows more urban, the need for nature in the city becomes more evident. Traditionally, urban dwellers viewed the natural world as something "out there," beyond the city limits—something to be avoided or tamed. But cities should be seen as human ecosystems where people interact with each other and other organisms as well as with their built and natural environments.

In the city, even glimpses of landscape are celebrated. As a result, Lake|Flato focuses on the spaces between buildings and emphasizes outdoor spaces in its urban houses. Rooms are organized around such spaces to provide light and privacy.

The converted San Antonio warehouse Dog Team Too Loft and Studio provides a strong example of the architects' commitment to urban renewal and urban landscapes. The organization of space resembles that found in a traditional hacienda. This urban hacienda includes a former alley that has become an entryway and a previous parking lot that is now a courtyard. These outdoor spaces help accentuate the transformation of this formerly gritty industrial building into a home and studio. These spaces also illustrate Lake|Flato's sustained commitment to landscape design, especially in urban areas.

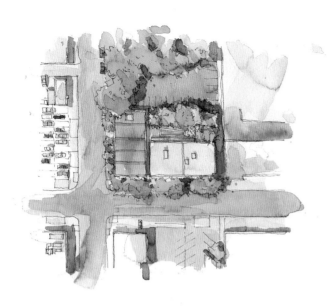

DOG TEAM TOO LOFT AND STUDIO
SAN ANTONIO, TEXAS

Located in a "light industrial" neighborhood in downtown San Antonio, Dog Team Too Loft and Studio presented a challenge: to celebrate the gritty quality of a former manufacturing complex and at the same time transform it into a comfortable oasis for living and working. And, as in the other structures in this collection, Lake|Flato treated the landscape and exterior spaces with as much respect as the interior spaces.

The overall layout is similar to that of a hacienda (an industrial one). The compound is entered via the old alley between the living and working structures and terminates in the new courtyard (a former service yard). New walls, plantings, and a raised "water trough" pool create an oasis-like setting in this hot industrial area. The living and working areas open directly to the courtyard and a third structure, a small storage building with walls removed, is the courtyard pavilion.

The original wood roof of the living loft, destroyed by a fire midway through construction, was replaced with a light steel north-facing sawtooth design, which stabilized the free-standing brick walls while also bringing abundant light into the living area. The light steel and smooth plywood design contrasts with the strongly textured wood structure in the work area.

"Before" images of existing buildings. In keeping with this building's industrial origins, the fire-damaged ceiling was replaced with a sawtooth roof that floods the interiors with north light.

The main living area, with its north-facing sawtooth roof and frosted-glass clerestories, has great natural light.

In the courtyard between the residential building and the office space, a sculptural lap
pool helps both to cool and to offset the compound's urban austerity.

Black painted concrete fiberboard set into the original brick structure preserves the building's industrial character from the outside while ensuring privacy and security for the owner on the inside.

The expansive loftlike space incorporates a compact work area.

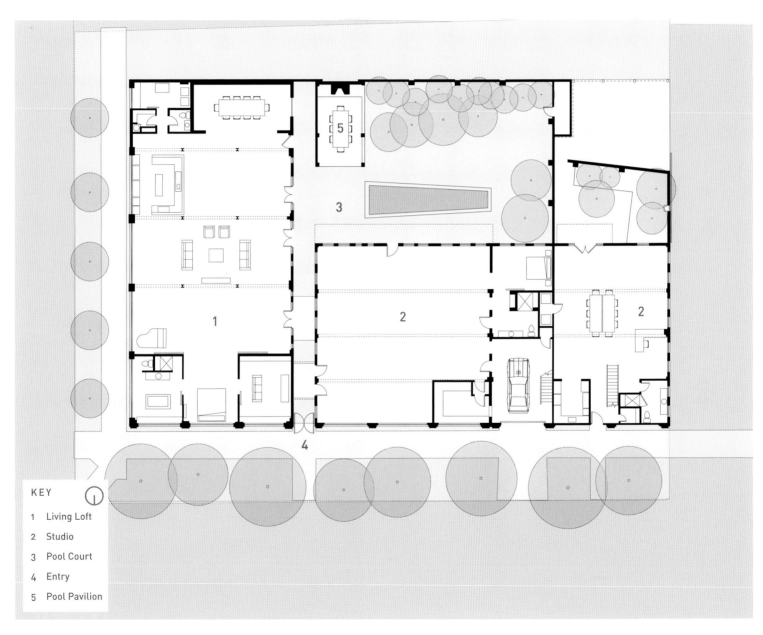

KEY ⊕

1 Living Loft

2 Studio

3 Pool Court

4 Entry

5 Pool Pavilion

BLUFFVIEW RESIDENCE
DALLAS, TEXAS

North Texas is known more for rolling prairies than for dramatic cliffs, but flowing into the Trinity River north of downtown Dallas is a small creek that cuts into a sheer limestone cliff. The Bluffview Residence is perched atop one of these rugged formations. Because the property is surrounded by other houses, the architects sought to minimize the presence of the neighbors while heightening the occupants' experience of the site's singular natural feature.

A garage and bedroom wing reaches out to the street and turns the traditional "front yard" into a private side courtyard with a series of stone steps, a "grand exterior hallway," that leads up to the main front door of the house. The house itself stops short of the cliff's edge, forming a more intimate forecourt framed by that edge.

This structured but naturally landscaped space acts as a foreground to the sweeping views down the creek.

The private rooms of the house are located in the long wing that rises up to the cliff's edge. The master suite occupies the highest point in the house, commanding a treetop view down to the creek below. The more public areas of the house occupy a low wing that runs parallel to the cliff. This public wing terminates in a living pavilion that overlooks a bend in the creek. Sliding glass walls and a continuous floor plane of stone connect this space to an outdoor patio built into the cliff's edge. A broad copper roof floats above all three of these elements and shades the expanses of glass and simple planes of natural hand-troweled stucco that form the house's exterior.

With its long, sloping roof, the bedroom wing extends to the street and creates a generous front courtyard for the pool and entry.

The open risers of the stairs allow light to pass through the space.

The living area projects out on the edge of the bluff to take advantage of the beautiful creek below.

A small balcony off the master bedroom provides a direct link into the canopy of trees that define the edge of the bluff overlooking the creek.

Perched on its own level, the master suite provides panoramic views of the rest of the house as well as the mature oak trees that dominate the site.

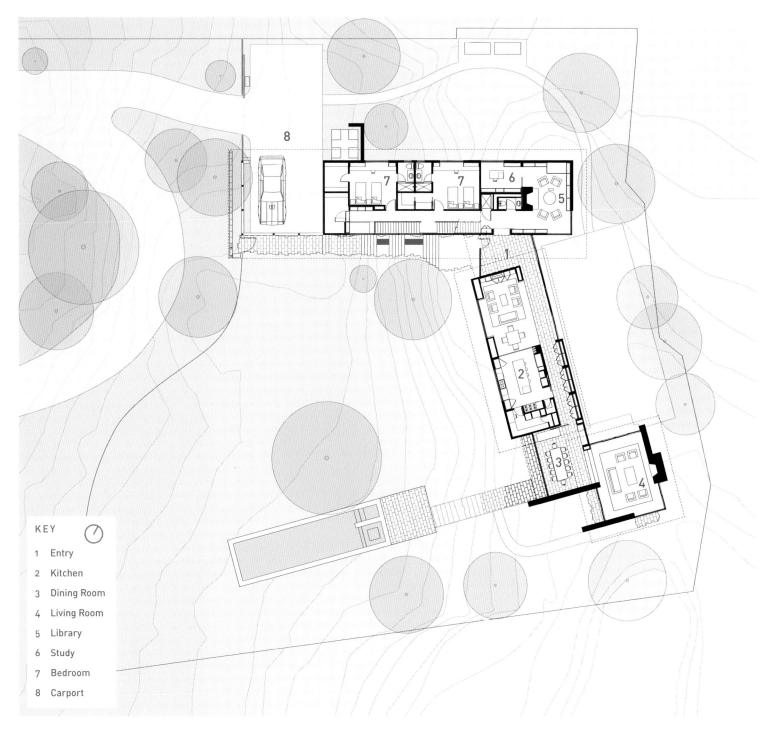

KEY

1 Entry

2 Kitchen

3 Dining Room

4 Living Room

5 Library

6 Study

7 Bedroom

8 Carport

BAYOU RESIDENCE
HOUSTON, TEXAS

Situated along a thickly forested bayou in a traditional residential area in Houston, this house edits out its neighbors while immersing itself in a uniquely shady pocket of the city. Designed in three parts, the house has a two-story living pavilion and entry court hinged between a public pavilion on the north and a shaded private pavilion along the bayou to the south. The voluminous steel and glass structure, with its light infill walls, invites the tall pine forest into the house. Large suspended rolling panels allow the owners the flexibility to change the spatial character of the house, shifting between an atmosphere of intimate living and one that promotes spacious entertaining.

A dialogue between steel frame, copper panels, stained stucco, and glass occurs throughout the house. The dynamic quality of the light filtering through the pine trees is further diffused by the cable-supported trellis and generous cantilevered overhangs. A screen porch adjacent to the kitchen helps merge the house with its natural setting.

The master suite, located on the second floor for privacy, is connected to the children's area by a bridge that traverses the two-story living room. Movable panels within the walls of the second floor unite the upstairs with the downstairs.

The house makes a nice transition from busy street to quiet woods: beginning with an intimate entry court, it then opens up to the dense pine trees and the nearby bayou.

A dialogue among steel frame, copper panels, stained stucco, and glass occurs throughout the house.

Large suspended rolling panels open and close to create alternately intimate living and spacious entertaining spaces.

Movable panels within the walls of the upstairs bedrooms unite the two levels of the house.

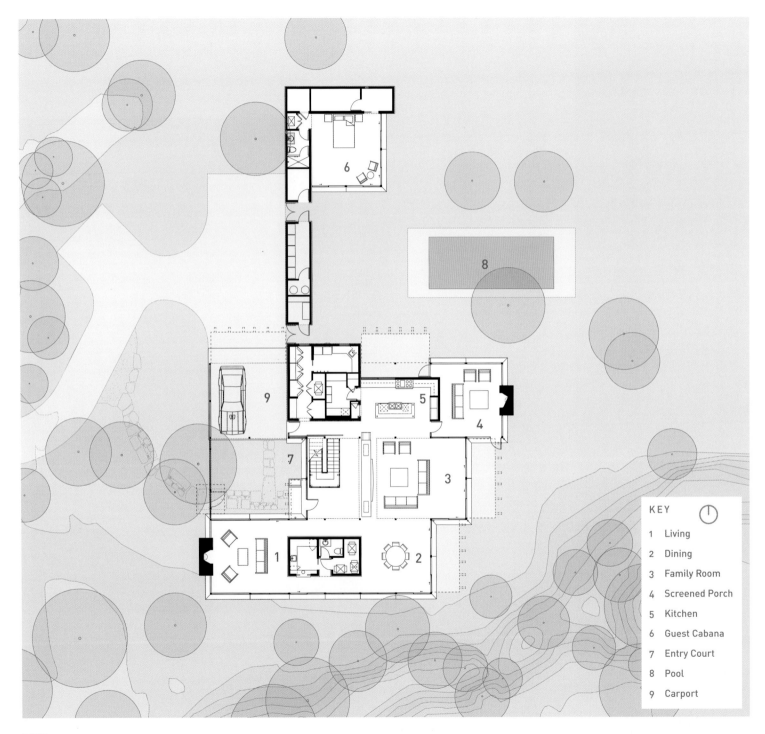

KEY

1   Living
2   Dining
3   Family Room
4   Screened Porch
5   Kitchen
6   Guest Cabana
7   Entry Court
8   Pool
9   Carport

The voluminous
steel and glass
structure invites
the tall pine forest
into the house.

WATER

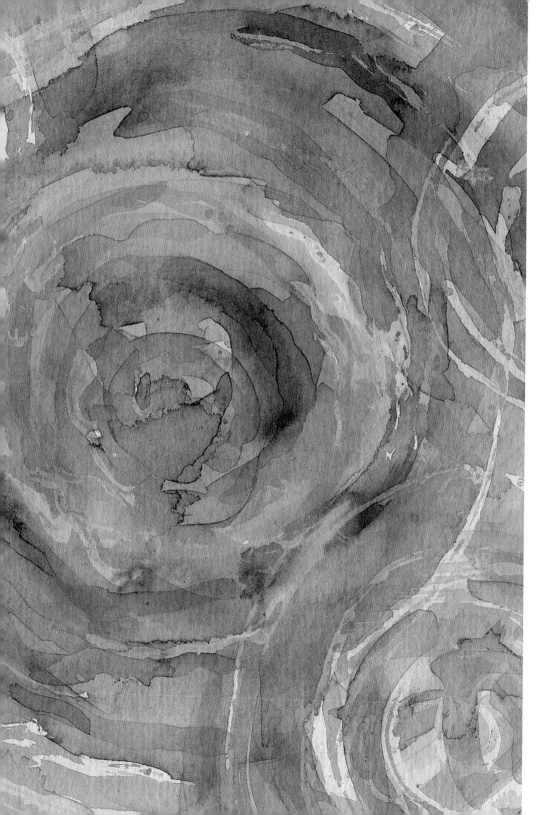

The interfaces between water and land form special, frequently fragile, environments. Álvaro Siza's Piscina da Maré (swimming pool on the sea) on the Atlantic coast at Matosinhos, Portugal, stands out as an inspired example of architecture at the edge of a continent where land meets water. As Siza observed, "There ripened a definite, undeniable feeling that architecture does not end at a specific point, but extends from object to space and thus—through the relation to space—finds its completion in nature."

In Texas, water-land interfaces are important design opportunities, as fresh water is precious. As a result, Lake|Flato celebrates water, often in spare ways that are reminiscent of a Japanese aesthetic. The architects arrange built structures to bring water closer to residents and to cool living spaces.

These water edges, where objects extend into space, play recurring roles in Lake|Flato's work. The Lake Austin House provides a nice example. Lake Austin resulted from one of the dams on the Colorado River, built to minimize flood damage and to provide drinking water for the region. The house, characterized by handsome wood structures that riff off the surrounding riparian woodlands, extends along a canal to the lake, finding its completion in the interplay between land and water.

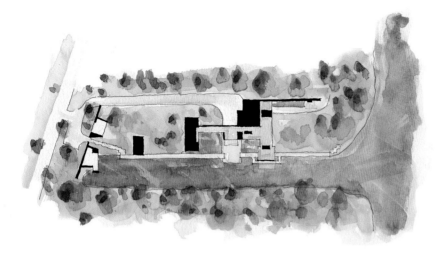

LAKE AUSTIN HOUSE
AUSTIN, TEXAS

The Colorado River, which bisects the city of Austin, is a precious resource that this house very much embraces. Located on a long narrow riverside lot, the house is conceived as a "floating fishing village" on the edge of a manmade canal, where a collection of small gabled buildings and boardwalks mask the line between land and water.

From the street, a massive limestone wall conceals a guesthouse and office and forms the entry for the riverside compound. Once inside the wall, a 200-foot-long boardwalk, the grand entry hall, connects a visitor to the rest of the rooms of the house. Bordering this walkway are several simple wood structures that house bedrooms and a study. These detached structures form a series of small courts and inlets off the canal, offering private gardens for the additional bedrooms.

The main living room sits at the end of this boardwalk. The entry to the house is a two-story screened boathouse pavilion that offers views up and down the canal and out to Lake Austin. By capturing breezes off the lake in the warmer months and through the use of a large fireplace in the cooler ones, the space can be used throughout much of the year.

After passing through this screened entry, a visitor sees a broad indoor corridor, animated by reflected light off the water, connecting the public and private areas of the house while also acting as a light-filled art gallery. Opposite the canal, a tall site wall of local limestone creates a private court for the master bedroom suite while dramatically framing views of the lake.

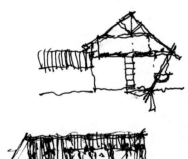

Aht
screen

storage
blocks

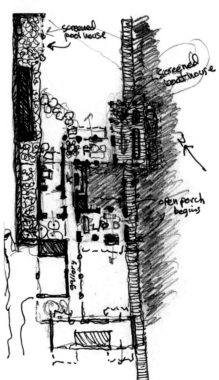

screened
pool house

Screened
boathouse

open porch
begins

Walking along a canal on
a long boardwalk, guests
arrive at the two-story
screened boathouse,
the home's "entry hall."
The arrangement of
buildings, linked by
a boardwalk, lends a
fishing village feel to the
property.

The screened
entry room,
surrounded
by water,
stays cool
even in the
hottest days
of summer.

251

A slat wall edits out a neighbor's
house while still allowing breezes
into the screened porch.

253

254

Light bounces off the adjacent
waterway and animates the houses
throughout the day.

Small side courtyards allow bathrooms to be closely connected with nature.

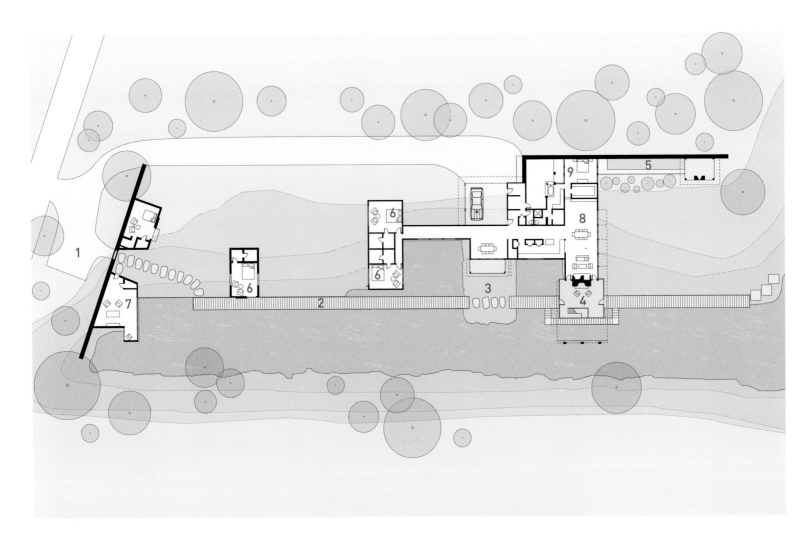

KEY

1   Entry Gate

2   Boardwalk

3   Island

4   Screened Boathouse

5   Pool

6   Guest Room

7   Studio

8   Living Room

9   Master Bedroom

The master bedroom, which shares a limestone wall with the adjacent lap pool, feels like a sleeping porch in the garden. The lap pool extends from the master suite to the lakeside cabana. Water, in this case, isn't simply something to enjoy from a picture window; it's an integral part of the architectural plan.

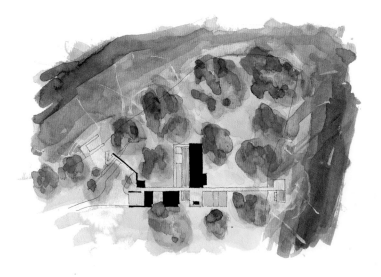

HOG PEN CREEK
AUSTIN, TEXAS

Originally developed in the 1940s as a series of lakefront cabins, the Hog Pen Creek residence embraces its informal, rural roots. The house is situated on the shady, tree-covered confluence of Hog Pen Creek and Lake Austin. The owners envisioned a place that would engage with the outdoors while providing accommodating spaces for their off-season training for triathlons.

Consistent with the lakefront cabin charm, the owners liked the idea of accessing much of the house from outdoor covered porches and walkways. The desire to have the main living area closely connected with the water, while respecting the floodplain and the majestic oaks on the property, suggested the design's stair-stepping boardwalk spine. The unique site plan includes the main house, a two-story dog run, and a guest cabin, all seamlessly stitched together by a grand boardwalk, making arrival by boat or by car an equally engaging experience.

The main living area, a two-story single-width volume with a master bedroom loft and porches on either end, takes advantage of the cool prevailing breezes and shade from the adjacent oak trees. The design of this large barnlike building, with its movable bedroom wall and "crow's-nest" office, allows the residence to be both intimate and social, effortlessly accommodating groups and individuals alike.

The wood slat-covered garage adds to the informality of this lakeside house.

The two-story dog-run entry porch
captures prevailing breezes off the lake.

The dining table was made from an old pecan tree that was felled by a heavy storm.

The kitchen, with its floating steel shelves, has a seamless connection with both the living area and the master bedroom loft above.

With a large, rolling barn door, the master bedroom can open completely to the downstairs living area and the lake views beyond.

A light steel bridge connects the crow's-nest office with the rest of the house.

The main living area and the lap pool share a common wall, allowing both swimming and light to animate the interiors.

The tall, screened room at the end of the living area enjoys dappled light from the majestic oaks.

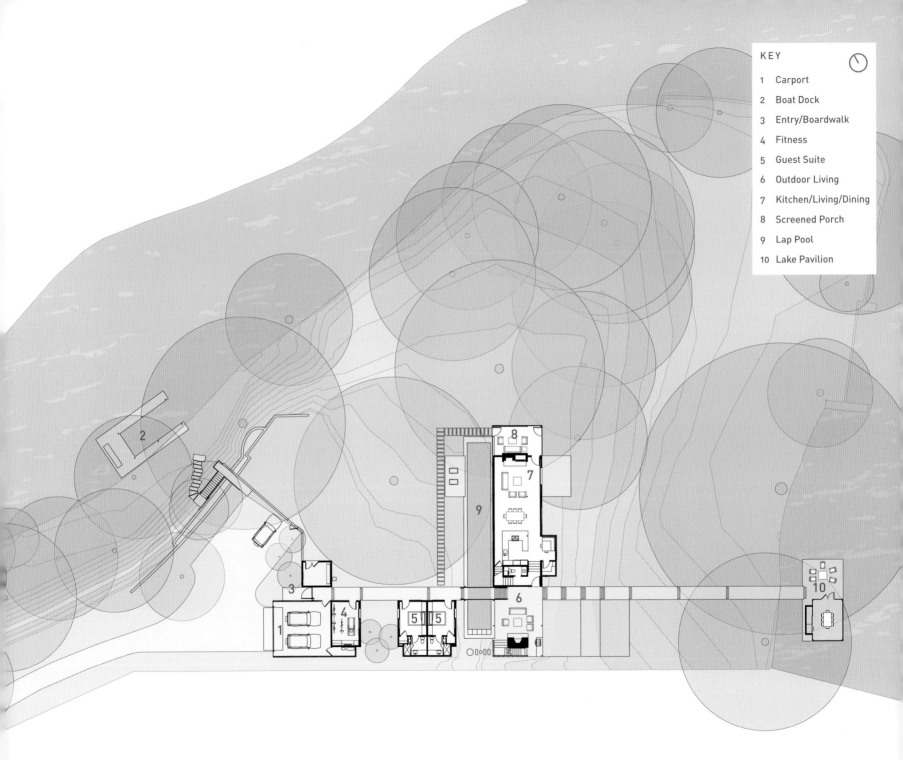

1   Carport

2   Boat Dock

3   Entry/Boardwalk

4   Fitness

5   Guest Suite

6   Outdoor Living

7   Kitchen/Living/Dining

8   Screened Porch

9   Lap Pool

10 Lake Pavilion

The stair-stepping boardwalk terminates at a screened boat pavilion that makes arrival by boat or by car an engaging experience.

277

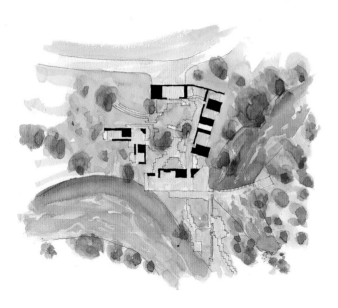

MILL SPRINGS RANCH
VANDERPOOL, TEXAS

Nestled at the confluence of two creeks on a sprawling Hill Country ranch, the Mill Springs homestead provides a water's-edge retreat in South Central Texas. The four building elements are organized around the site of the original ranch house and dam, resulting in a courtyard shaded by mature pecan trees and an intimate connection to the cool spring-fed creeks.

The main living area aligns with the geometry of the existing dam and provides dynamic views of the creeks and the valley landforms they have shaped over time. The family bedroom wing serves as a mediating element between the creek and the natural valley landscape.

Focusing on the main creek and pecan grove, the bedrooms leverage the two most treasured elements in the harsh Texas climate: water and shade.

Conceptually, the house is a series of artifacts linked in spirit to the original dam. Masonry walls built of locally quarried limestone anchor each space to the original ranch layout and orient the rooms to cooling breezes, landscape elements, and beautiful views. Light steel and glass walls with large sliding doors provide either an immediate connection to the outdoors or complete the enclosure of the spaces in response to the varying weather conditions.

The living area has large, rolling doors and drop-down screens that allow the room to enjoy the views, breezes, and light from its creekside location.

The recessed kitchen and stone fireplace create intimate spaces within the expansive living area.

The screened guest living area has
an intimate connection with the
outdoors.

The stone walls of the bedrooms reach out into the landscape and, with their rolling glass doors, connect the guest with nature.

Breaks in the stone walls connect the courtyard to the creek beyond.

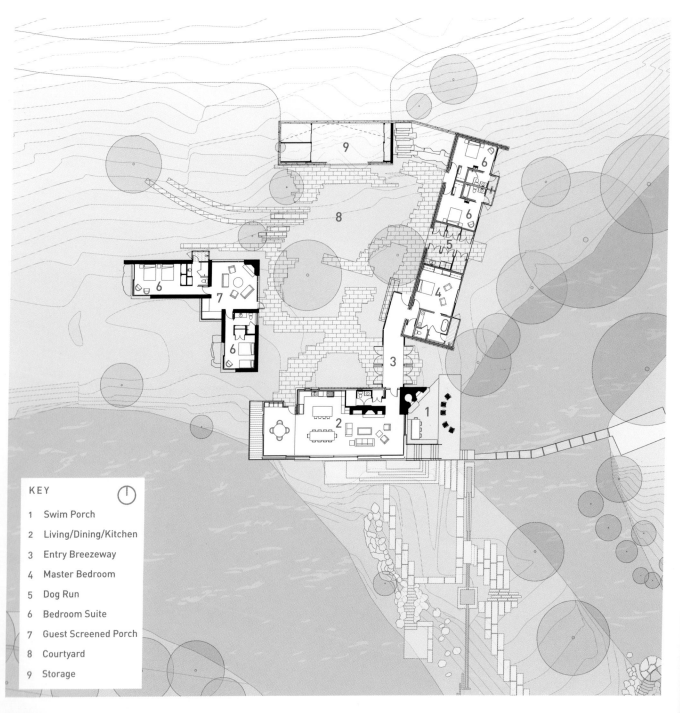

KEY

1   Swim Porch

2   Living/Dining/Kitchen

3   Entry Breezeway

4   Master Bedroom

5   Dog Run

6   Bedroom Suite

7   Guest Screened Porch

8   Courtyard

9   Storage

PROJECT CREDITS

INTRODUCTION

PHOTOGRAPHY: Alamo Cement House, Hester + Hardaway Photographers; La Barronena Ranch, Lake|Flato; Airbarns, Dawn Laurel Photography; El Tule Ranch, Scott Frances; Chandler Ranch, Tim Hursley Photography; Hill Country Jacal, Leigh Christian; House of Light, Hester + Hardaway Photographers; Elm Court Residence, Scott Frances, Hester + Hardaway Photographers; Lasater Residence, Craig Blackmon; Lucky Boy Ranch, Hester + Hardaway Photographers; Broadford Farm Pavilion, Lake|Flato; Cloud 9, Chris Cooper

DESIGN TEAM: David Lake, Ted Flato, Karla Greer, Brian Korte, Robert Trinidad, Joseph Benjamin, Graham Martin, John Grable, Kenny Brown, Eric Buck, Jay Pigford, Joaquin Escamilla, Ahbeek Sarkar, Javier Sartorio

BARTLIT RESIDENCE | 2001 | 10000 FT²

DESIGN TEAM: David Lake, Karla Greer, Bill Aylor, Robert Trinidad, Isabel Mijangos, Javier Huerta, Francisco Lopez

COLLABORATORS: General Contractor, Beck and Associates Inc.; Structural Engineer, Datum Engineers; Landscape Architect, Kings Creek Landscaping; Lighting Designer, Fisher Marantz Stone; Interiors, Gregga Jordan Smieszny Inc.

PUBLICATIONS: *Architectural Digest, Innovative Home, Texas Architect, Case di vacanza, Essence of Home, Living Outside the House, Stone Houses, Sustainable Homes, House: American Houses for the New Century, 100 of the World's Best Houses*

PHOTOGRAPHY: Hester + Hardaway Photographers, Frank Ooms Photography, David O. Marlow/*Architectural Digest*; © Condé Nast

BAYOU RESIDENCE | 2004 | 9000 FT²

DESIGN TEAM: Ted Flato, Karla Greer, Billy Johnson, Tenna Florian, Heather DeGrella, Joe Neely

COLLABORATORS: General Contractor, Renaissance Builders, Inc.; Structural Engineer, Consulting Engineers; Landscape Architect, McDugald Steele Landscape; Lighting Designer, Architectural Lighting Consultants; Interiors, Peggy McGaughy

PUBLICATIONS: *Architecture Magazine, Houston House and Home*

PHOTOGRAPHY: Frank Ooms Photography

BLUFFVIEW RESIDENCE | 2008 | 6700 FT²

DESIGN TEAM: Ted Flato, Karla Greer, Billy Johnson, Brantley Hightower, Tobin Smith, Kim Monroe

COLLABORATORS: General Contractor, Sebastian Construction Group; Structural Engineer, R. L. Goodson; Landscape Architect, MESA Design Group; Lighting Designer, Architectural Lighting Consultants; Interiors, Nancy Leib

PUBLICATIONS: *Western Interiors*

PHOTOGRAPHY: Steven Vaughan, Matthew Millman

BROWN RESIDENCE | 2009 | 4643 FT²

DESIGN TEAM: Ted Flato, Brian Comeaux, Parrish Kyle

COLLABORATORS: General Contractor, The Construction Zone Ltd.; Structural Engineer, Datum Engineers Inc.; Landscape Architect, Tonnesen Inc. Landscape Architecture; Lighting Designer, Lighting Consultants; Interiors, Robyn Menter Design Associates

PUBLICATIONS: *Modern Steel, Texas Architect, Pure Luxury: World's Best Houses, Bespoke, 21st Century Homes, Western Art & Architecture*

PHOTOGRAPHY: Bill Timmerman

CROSS TIMBERS RANCH | 2010 | 8000 FT²

DESIGN TEAM: Ted Flato, Bill Aylor, Ryan Jones, Nate Campbell

COLLABORATORS: General Contractor, Duecker Construction; Structural Engineer, Structural Design Consulting; Landscape Architect, Kings Creek Landscaping; Lighting Designer, Lake|Flato Architects; Interiors, Harry J. Crouse Design

PUBLICATIONS: *Texas Architect*, *Garden & Gun*

PHOTOGRAPHY: Frank Ooms Photography

CUTTING HORSE RANCH | 2009 | 175 ACRES

DESIGN TEAM: Ted Flato, Bill Aylor, Ryan Jones, Lewis McNeel, Albert Condarco

COLLABORATORS: General Contractor, Lincoln Builders; Structural Engineer, Datum Engineers Inc.; Landscape Architect, MESA Design Group; Lighting Designer, Lake|Flato Architects; Equestrian Consultant, GH2 Gralla

PHOTOGRAPHY: Frank Ooms Photography

DOG TEAM TOO LOFT AND STUDIO | 2001 | 12000 FT²

DESIGN TEAM: Ted Flato, Bob Harris, Heather DeGrella

COLLABORATORS: General Contractor, Bill Cox; Structural Engineer, Steve Persyn Consulting Engineers; Landscape Architect, Lake|Flato Architects; Interior Designer, Jill Giles Design

PUBLICATIONS: *Architectural Digest*, *Innovative Home*, *Metropolitan Home*, *Residential Architect*, *Texas Architect*, *Sustainable Homes*, *Home*, *Live/Work: Working at Home/Living at Work*, *The Green House: New Directions in Sustainable Architecture*

PHOTOGRAPHY: Chris Cooper, Mary Nichols/*Architectural Digest*; © Condé Nast

DESERT HOUSE | 2009 | 6500 FT²

DESIGN TEAM: David Lake, Bill Aylor, Nate Campbell, Ryan Jones, Brian Korte

COLLABORATORS: General Contractor, McDowell Construction, Inc.; Structural Engineer, Hands Engineering, Inc.; Landscape Design, Chamisa Landscaping; Lighting Designer, George Sexton Associates; Civil Engineer, RME Santa Fe Engineering

PUBLICATIONS: *Pure Luxury: World's Best Houses*, *Wallpaper Magazine*

PHOTOGRAPHY: Frank Ooms Photography

DUNNING RESIDENCE | 2003 | 4500 FT²

DESIGN TEAM: Ted Flato, Andrew Herdeg, Roy Schweers

COLLABORATORS: General Contractor, Denman Construction; Structural Engineer, Red Mountain Engineers; Landscape Architect, Julie Berman Design; Lighting Designer, Architectural Lighting Consultants; Interiors, Sarah Dunning Design Studio

PUBLICATIONS: *Western Interiors*, *Residential Architect*

PHOTOGRAPHY: Tim Hursley Photography, Dominique Vorillon Photography

HILLSIDE HOUSE | 2011 | 4234 FT² AC/ 3288 FT² NON-AC

DESIGN TEAM: Ted Flato, Karla Greer, Jonathan Smith, Kim Drennan, Mia Frietz

COLLABORATORS: General Contractor, Pinnelli Construction Company, Inc.; Structural Engineer, Datum Engineering; Landscape Architect, Garden Design Studio; Lighting Designer, Lighting Consultants Inc.; Interiors, Terry Hunziker

PUBLICATIONS: *Architectural Digest*

PHOTOGRAPHY: Aaron Leitz Photography

HOG PEN CREEK | 2013 | 2836 FT² AC/ 4007 FT² NON-AC

DESIGN TEAM: Ted Flato, Brian Comeaux, Raina Tilden, Rebecca Bruce

COLLABORATORS: General Contractor, Don Crowell Builders; Structural Engineer, Datum Engineering; Landscape Architect, Garden Design Studio; Lighting, Studio Lumina; Interiors, ABODE | Fern Santini Design

PHOTOGRAPHY: Casey Dunn Photography

LAKE AUSTIN HOUSE | 2003 | 6000 FT²

DESIGN TEAM: Ted Flato, Bill Aylor, Daryl Ohlenbusch

COLLABORATORS: General Contractor, Thompson + Hansen; Structural Engineer, Lundy and Associates; Landscape Architect, Thompson + Hansen; Lighting Designer, Lake|Flato Architects; Interiors, Stonefox Interiors

PUBLICATIONS: *Architectural Digest*, *Residential Architect Magazine*, *Tribeza*, *Modern Painters*, *The New 100 Houses x 100 Architects*

PHOTOGRAPHY: Hester + Hardaway Photographers, Patrick Wong, Robert Reck/*Architectural Digest*; © Condé Nast

LAKE TAHOE RESIDENCE | 2003 | 4700 FT²

DESIGN TEAM: David Lake, Billy Johnson, Tenna Florian, Heather DeGrella, Joe Neely

COLLABORATORS: General Contractor, Q+D Construction; Structural Engineer, Datum Engineers Inc.; Landscape Architect, Kings Creek Landscaping; Lighting Designer, Lighting Consultants Inc.

PUBLICATIONS: *Architectural Record*, *Texas Architect*, *Tahoe Quarterly*

PHOTOGRAPHY: Jeff Dow

LC RANCH | 2009 | 4055 FT²

DESIGN TEAM: David Lake, Bill Aylor, Trey Rabke

COLLABORATORS: General Contractor, Yellowstone Traditions; Structural Engineer, Datum Engineers, Inc.; Landscape Architect, Linda Iverson; Lighting Designer, Lake|Flato Architects/Madeline Stuart; Interiors, Madeline Stuart & Associates

PUBLICATIONS: *Residential Architect*, *Architectural Digest*

PHOTOGRAPHY: Frank Ooms Photography, Joshua McHugh

MILL SPRINGS RANCH | 2012 | 4234 FT² AC/3288 FT² NON-AC

DESIGN TEAM: Ted Flato, Steve Raike, Laura Kaupp, Chris Krajcer

COLLABORATORS: General Contractor, Duecker Construction, Inc.; Structural Engineer, Datum Engineers, Inc.; Landscape Architect, Ten Eyck Landscape Architecture; Lighting Designer, Studio Lumina; Mechanical, Southwest Mechanical; Interior Design, Poet Interiors

PHOTOGRAPHY: Casey Dunn Photography

PORCH HOUSE | 2010 | 1600 FT² AC/ 1400 FT² NON-AC

DESIGN TEAM: Ted Flato, Bill Aylor, Roy Schweers, Wade Miller, Richard McFarland, Heather Kyle

COLLABORATORS: General Contractor, Duecker Construction, Inc.; Structural Engineer, RCS Enterprises; Landscape Architect, TenEyck Landscape Architects

PUBLICATIONS: *Modern Luxe Interiors*, *Mountain Living*, *Residential Architect*, *Southern Living*

PHOTOGRAPHY: Frank Ooms Photography, Kenny Braun, Casey Dunn Photography

STORY POOL HOUSE | 2010 | 2375 FT²

DESIGN TEAM: Ted Flato, Karla Greer, Jennifer Young, Cameron Smith, Brantley Hightower

COLLABORATORS: General Contractor, Duecker Construction, Inc.; Structural Engineer, Jack Harrison P.E.; Landscape Design, Canyon Creek Maintenance; Lighting Designer, Brown Design Consultants; Interiors, Joey Story and Sara Story Design

PUBLICATIONS: *Dwell Outside*

PHOTOGRAPHY: Casey Dunn Photography

TOUCHE PASS HOUSE | 2007 | 7600 FT²

DESIGN TEAM: Ted Flato, Karla Greer, Tobin Smith

COLLABORATORS: General Contractor, Stocker & Allaire; Structural Engineer, Datum Engineers Inc.; Landscape Architect, Joni Janecki + Associates; Lighting Designer, Lighting Consultants LLC; Interiors, Emily Summers

PUBLICATIONS: *New York Times*, *Dwell*

PHOTOGRAPHY: Frank Ooms Photography, Sara Remington

ARTWORK

CHAPTER WATERCOLORS: Matt Morris, FAIA

PLAN WATERCOLORS: Matt Morris, FAIA

SITE PLANS/DIAGRAMS: David Ericsson, Jacqueline Fisher, Matthew Hlavinka, Thomas Johnston, Jelisa Blumberg, Hillary Whites, Joseph Dugan, Hellen Anyango-Awino, Sam H. Pepper

FLAKELATO PAINTING: Malou Flato

SPECIAL THANKS: "Lines on Green Land" by Matt Morris, from the collection of Laura Kaupp

GUY MARTIN has written for numerous magazines, including *Condé Nast Traveler*, *Garden & Gun*, the (London) *Observer*, the (London) *Sunday Telegraph*, and the *New Yorker*. A native of Athens, Alabama, a small cotton town in the Tennessee Valley, he grew up in a house designed by the architect Paul Rudolph, who had been friends with his parents. Martin lives in Berlin, Germany, and New York City.

FREDERICK STEINER, FASLA, is the Henry M. Rockwell Chair in Architecture and Dean of the School of Architecture at the University of Texas at Austin. His most recent books include *Design for a Vulnerable Planet*, *The Essential Ian McHarg: Writings on Design and Nature*, *Planning and Urban Design Standards: Student Edition* (with Kent Butler), and *Human Ecology: Following Nature's Lead*.

COVER Lake Austin House, Austin, Texas.
Front: Photo by Hester + Hardaway.
Back: Photo by Patrick Y. Wong/atelierwong.com.